Lucid Dreaming for Beginners

What You Need to Know About Controlling Your Dreams to Improve Your Sleep and Creativity

Your Free Gift (only available for a limited time)

Thanks for getting this book! If you want to learn more about various spirituality topics, then join Mari Silva's community and get a free guided meditation MP3 for awakening your third eye. This guided meditation mp3 is designed to open and strengthen ones third eye so you can experience a higher state of consciousness. Simply visit the link below the image to get started.

https://spiritualityspot.com/meditation

Contents

Introduction

We all dream, and our dreams can be happy, exhilarating, exciting, frightening, or intriguing. Our unique ability to dream has been a fascinating aspect that science has been trying to explore since the dawn of civilization. Dreams are like live-action movies, which signify a lot of things. In your dreams, the sky is the limit, and there isn't anything you cannot try or do. You can be a magician, explore your wildest ideas, and delve into your subconscious.

Do you always remember your dreams? Chances are, you often forget about them the moment you open your eyes.

With lucid dreaming, you can recollect your dreams and even control them. Lucid dreaming is a fascinating concept which teaches you to become consciously aware of yourself while in dreamland. It makes you the writer, director, actor, and producer of your own play. If you ever thought about exploring some of your ideas but lack the confidence to do it, lucid dreaming will come in handy. Lucid dreaming is the key to discovering your inner self – the world within you – and your subconscious. From exploring your goals and fantasies to living your dreams, you can do it all.

In this book, you will learn about dreams and their meaning, about lucid dreaming, and the different benefits it offers. You will also learn about the relationship between astral projection, shamanic journeying, and lucid dreaming, some tips to prepare for learning more about lucid dreaming, and steps to prepare for an enhanced lucid dreaming experience.

Apart from that, you will discover various lucid dreaming techniques ideal for beginners and some advanced techniques, too. In this book, you will find practical and simple tips for exploring the lucid dreamscape, meeting spirit guides, and how to protect yourself during lucid dreams. Some helpful tips about avoiding certain mistakes when you are lucid dreaming are included in this book.

So, are you ready to learn more about all this? Are you excited to start your personal journey into the world of lucid dreams? If yes, let's get started without further ado!

Chapter One: What Are Dreams?

Dreams are a mystery to us, and scientists and psychologists have long been studying them to try to understand more. They might seem weird, strange, or even terrifying, but your dreams have a meaning. It is believed that your dreams help to maintain your physical and psychological health. There are many theories on dreams that have stated that dreams do have a purpose, but some theories state that dreams may have no purpose at all. Once you learn about lucid dreaming, your perception of dreams will change.

Psychologists have conducted thorough research on dreams. Their research dates back to the early 1900s, and they have performed psychological analyses of people's dreams for many years. The psychologists analyzed the dreams of their patients in dream laboratories and used the information they obtained to develop their theories. Sigmund Freud held out the first theory of dreams; he claimed that dreams only helped the person having them sleep well through the night. Freud also believed that people only had dreams when they were hungry, had a sexual urge, or needed to use the washroom. His theory was later contradicted when someone claimed that a person dreams at least five times when he is in the REM (Rapid Eye Movement) stage of his sleep cycle.

Carl Jung stated the next famous theory. He was an ardent follower of Freud, but he believed there was a different purpose behind dreams, and broke away from the Freudian theory to state a new theory. He claimed that a person had dreams to compensate for the parts of his total personality or psyche that were underdeveloped when he was awake.

Calvin Hall contradicted this theory with his own. To confirm his theory, he asked his students to maintain a dream journal for two weeks. He believed that a person would always represent himself in his dream. This meant that a person who is an introvert when he is awake is also an introvert in his dreams.

Other dream theorists believe dreams are the solutions to all our problems. They believe dreams only occur when a person is facing an unsolvable problem in life. Many psychologists tried to obtain evidence to back this theory, and it was during this research that they were finally able to establish the use of dreams based these on different cultural beliefs.

Why Do We Dream?

Freud had claimed that every person was a poet, intentionally or not, and that dreams were much like poetry. Poets use muses or experiences in their lives to write, and they express their emotions through poems. In the same way, you create images and situations in your dreams, and when you combine them with various events in your life, you elicit an emotional response within yourself. Dreams are stories that run through your unconscious or subconscious mind, and Freud believed these were not based on logic. Dreams are like motion pictures starring our emotions, fears, desires, and everything else buried in the subconscious.

Let us assume you argued with your friend this morning, and you were unable to get your point across. When you have a dream later tonight, you may find yourself in the same situation but arguing differently, and perhaps making your point quite well. Dreams help you change the outcome of situations that have already occurred. Events in your dream are based on the thoughts and emotions in your subconscious.

Another example can be one where you are taking an exam. Before the exam season starts, you may have many dreams where you either ace or fail the examination. You may have such a dream either because you want to be the valedictorian or because you fear examinations. When you are wide-awake, you cannot study for the test because you are worried about how you will fare. This still does not help us understand why we dream, but there are five theories regarding that.

Theory One: Practice Responses

Did you ever dream about falling off a cliff, fighting an enemy, or being chased by a dog? Well, you are not the first person to have such a dream. You tend to have such dreams during your REM sleep because your amygdala, the part of your brain that stimulates your fight-or-flight response, works at its peak. Antti Revonsuo, a Finnish cognitive scientist, stated that people dream only during their REM sleep.

It is during your REM sleep that your brain works as if it perceives danger because the amygdala is functioning at its peak. The part of your brain that controls your motor ability also works at its peak, and you may not be moving your limbs when you are asleep, but you can still have a dream where you are taking a stroll down the beach or fighting for your life. Antti proved that dreams are your stage, and that is where your brain rehearses a potential threat. You rehearse your reactions – both physical and emotional – during your dreams. It is for this reason some people kick in their sleep or wake up crying.

Theory Two: Sifting Through Memories

Your brain limits the number of images it stores in your conscious memory. If you remembered every image from every event that happened in life, your brain would be clogged with irrelevant information. Your brain sorts through your memories in your subconscious mind and tries to identify those memories it should store and those it should get rid of. If you want to understand this better, think about how the mind works in the movie *Inside Out*. In that movie, a group of people "lived" inside the brain, looking at their subconscious memories and tossing them out when they turned grey. This is exactly how your mind works. There is no team, but your brain does flush out any unwanted memories and images.

Similarly, your brain segregates the memories through your dreams. Matt Wilson, a professor at MIT's Center for Learning and Memory, strongly backs this theory. In his experiments on rats, he put them in a maze throughout the day and monitored their neuron patterns. Wilson paid close attention to their neuron patterns during their REM sleep and discovered that the patterns were the same as those when the rats were running in the maze. He claimed that the brain uses dreams to identify the worthiness of a memory. Your sleep turns all the information you have into strong memories, helping you make decisions in the future.

Theory Three: Dreaming is Defragmentation

When you buy a new laptop or desktop, the first thing you do is separate your drives. You create the number of drives you want in the space provided by the device. In the same way, your brain also tries to identify the importance of all your memories. Francis Crick and Graeme Mitchison claimed that a person dreamed in order to forget. They meant that your brain tries to identify whether the data it contains, in the form of memories, is useful or not. It tries to establish a connection between your memories, attempting to identify those it should keep in the active memory, and those it should move to your subconscious memory. Your brain uses this method to go through your memories to identify those connections that are important and those that are not.

Theory Four: Your Personal Psychotherapist

Ernest Hartmann, a doctor at Tufts, proposed that dreams help us confront those emotions we refuse to acknowledge. He focused on what people learn when they dream. He stated the theory that your brain uses images and a sequence of events to help you face those emotions your conscious mind is scared to look at. When you dream, you deal with all your difficult emotions in a safe place, which is similar to psychotherapy. You can consider dreams to be your therapists, and your bed is the therapeutic couch. You observe all your emotions and thoughts, and let your brain tell you what you should do to prevent an emotional imbalance. Through your dreams, you learn to accept certain truths that you would have never been able to accept consciously.

Theory Five: No Meaning At All

We mentioned earlier that some people now believe there is no meaning to your dreams. Modern theorists have argued that the brain fires images at random, and some of these situations may not have anything to do with something that occurred when you were conscious. Your dreams are like a film where you are the hero, and the story is not dependent on your life.

Some Facts

Did you ever experience any terrifying, weird, fascinating, exciting, and fun dreams? Well, we have all experienced a variety of dreams, but might not remember most of them. Before we learn to look at how you can remember them, let us look at some interesting facts about dreams.

Everyone Dreams

Yes, everyone, including men, women, babies, and even animals, dream. People who claim to have a dreamless sleep are mistaken. They dream, too, but do not remember them when they wake up. Psychologists believe there is enough evidence to prove that everyone dreams, and a person may have more than ten dreams each night. They also found that each dream lasts only for ten minutes, but you may have some dreams that last for more than forty-five minutes. Over a lifetime the average person will dream for a total of more than six years.

You Cannot Remember All of Your Dreams

Have you ever had this wonderful dream and wanted to remember it in the morning? You may have even told yourself to remember it during the dream or a half-awake moment immediately thereafter, but you wake up in the morning with only a feeling that you have forgotten something wonderful. Allan Hobson, a dream researcher, stated that you forget close to 95 percent of your dreams a few minutes after you wake up. He scanned the brains of his subjects while they slept, and found that the frontal lobe of the brain, essential in storing memory, was inactive when they were dreaming.

You May Have Colors in Your Dreams

Many psychologists believe that at least eighty percent of your dreams have a lot of colors. Some people claim they only dream in black and white. But if you were to wake someone up during their REM sleep and ask them to choose a color that they just saw in their dream, they would pick any color other than black or white.

You Can Control Your Dreams

That does sound fascinating, does it not? People can use various lucid dreaming techniques to control their dreams. When you master this technique, you will be aware of the fact that you are dreaming, although you are asleep. Psychologists believe that at least five out of ten people have had lucid dreams, but they are not aware of it. There are quite a few individuals who have frequent lucid dreams. The concept of lucid dreaming is covered in detail later in the book.

Dreams Can Paralyze You

During your REM sleep, the part of your brain that deals with motor functions is latent. You may have had a dream where you were being chased by a dog and woken up terrified. You may have wanted to move your muscles to snap out of the dream, but you found it hard or even impossible. This is called sleep paralysis, and it is not permanent. You may feel paralyzed even after you wake up, but this feeling only lasts no more than ten minutes. There may have been dreams in which you were flailing your arms around and screaming, or felt your breath catching in your throat. During dream paralysis, none of those actions actually happen.

Dream Interpretation

Carl Jung is one of the founding fathers of dream interpretation, and he believed that dreams were like a window into your unconscious mind. Jung claimed that when a person was dreaming, he was identifying different solutions to problems that he had faced or might face when he was conscious.

Jung was an ardent follower of Freud, but he disagreed with his theories and began to research dream interpretation. He said that only the dreamer could interpret their dreams. He said that certain common symbols could be interpreted, but only the dreamer could interpret the other symbols that are unique to him. There are dream dictionaries describing the meaning of the objects frequently found in dreams. The next section of this chapter helps you identify how you can interpret your dreams!

Do your dreams have a hidden meaning?

When you have had a dream, first ask yourself whether that dream is of any significance to you. If it is, you will have to ask yourself if the dream has any meaning to it.

Have you ever had a dream in which you were falling off a cliff? You might have been rolling off the bed at the very same time. Your subconscious mind is conveying a message to you in the form of a dream, telling you that you are rolling off your bed. Dreams that are related to the physical environment you are in have little or no hidden meaning. For instance, if you were to have a dream where a loud noise was being made, it may not have any drastic impact on your life because it is just a reflection of the fact that a noisy truck is passing by, or there is thunder in the distance. Your subconscious mind often incorporates the happenings in your immediate physical environment into your dreams. For instance, you might hear the doorbell ringing in your dream. In reality, the baby monitor might have been buzzing.

Your subconscious is sending you a message asking you to wake up because of the noise.

Have you ever had a nightmare after watching a horror movie? The emotions and fear that you had experienced while watching the movie can be translated into your dreams. This is why external circumstances that bring about a certain emotional response from you have a strong and deep impact on your dreams.

Certain elements are often found in the dreams of most people. These dreams elicit a wide range of emotions, and can be interpreted easily.

Common Dreams and their Interpretation

The most common dreams every individual has had on numerous occasions are discussed here. Irrespective of whether it's getting lost or falling, each dream conveys a specific meaning.

Falling Dreams

Falling dreams are very common dreams. They are memorable dreams. These dreams indicate that you are afraid of losing or letting go. They also indicate that you are anxious about failing after success.

Nude Dreams

There are times when you might have had dreams where you found it difficult to cover yourself fully. If you have had this dream, it shows that you are afraid of letting yourself close to anyone. You are vulnerable when exposed to others.

Floating Dreams

In these dreams, you find yourself becoming weightless and flying throughout the world your dream has created. Such dreams symbolize a deep desire for freedom.

Danger

These dreams commonly have a danger that might be approaching you. You are usually rendered helpless since you are unable to move. Such dreams might be indicators that there is a danger that might come in your way. They help you identify a solution via your dream.

Chasing Dreams

Dreams in which a known or unknown pursuer is chasing you indicate that you are feeling threatened in life.

Exam Dreams

This dream is often considered to be a mirrored dream. In these dreams, you are usually dreaming about being tested. These dreams signify self-evaluation. The questions in the examination are commonly related to various aspects of your personality.

Common dreams are a fascinating subject for researchers. They have found that every human being, even from different cultures, has experienced a variety of these dreams. Some psychologists have a theory that states human beings have these common dreams due to the interactions that they have with other people regularly.

How to Analyze Your Dreams

The biggest myth about the analysis of dreams is that there are rules that need to be followed word for word. This is, however, false, since every person is different. Jeffrey Sumber, a clinical psychotherapist, said that a dream could only be understood when an individual understood himself better. There are, however, certain guidelines that you can follow to make it easier for you to understand and analyze your dreams.

Maintain a Record of Your Dreams

The first step toward analyzing your dreams is to make a note of them. Sumber also said that when you note down your dreams, you are drawing the content out of your unconscious. If you feel that you cannot remember a dream, keep a journal by your bed and make a note saying, 'No dreams to record.' You will notice that within a span of two weeks, you start remembering your dreams!

Identify Your Emotions in the Dream

Ask yourself questions. Identify whether you were scared or remorseful or happy in the dream. Are those feelings dormant or active when you wake up in the morning? The final question should be whether or not you were comfortable with those feelings.

Identify the Elements of Your Dream

You might feature in your dreams in multiple ways. You will find a clear distinction between yourself and your characters in the dream. You will have to understand your emotions toward your characters in your dreams, too. They may be recurring elements in your dreams. Make a note of those and pay close attention to them while interpreting your dream.

You are the Expert!

You now have a number of dreams written down. When you are starting out, you may use a dream dictionary, which will help you identify the meaning behind every element in your dream. But you have to remember that you know yourself better than anyone else. So, let your subconscious guide you to help you understand and interpret your dreams. You will gain a lot of information about the memories stored in your unconscious.

By using the different guidelines discussed in this section, you can get a better understanding of yourself and the reasons for your dreams.

Chapter Two: Lucid Dreaming

Have you ever had a dream where you were a wizard or a bird? Have you dreamt that you were soaring through the clouds and shooting across the sky like Superman? Have you ever imagined a vacation on a Caribbean island? Remember any dream that ranks as one of your favorites; did you find it any less enjoyable because it was a dream? No, you enjoyed every bit of it. Now. how would you feel if you could control your dreams?

As mentioned in the earlier chapters, lucid dreaming is the method by which an individual is aware that he is dreaming. If a person is in a lucid dream, he can exercise the power of the dream. He can change the direction of the dream and also change the objects and entities in the dream. For instance, if you are in a lucid dream, and your environment is your bedroom, you can make your bed fly. You can create an entirely different universe behind the door to your bedroom. It is like you are writing your very own comic book. You can create your very own stage in your dreams and rehearse for a play or for a confrontation that you might have the next day.

History of Lucid Dreaming

The ancient practice of Yoga Nidra helps dreamers become more aware of what they are dreaming. This was a common practice of various people following Buddhist traditions. Some texts also show that lucid dreaming was a technique practiced in ancient Greece. For instance, Aristotle, the famous Greek philosopher, said, "Often when one is asleep, there is something in consciousness which declares that what then presents itself is but a dream." It was also believed that Galen, a physician from Pergamon, asked his patients to use this technique to help them overcome different problems and situations in life.

Lucid dreaming dates as far back as 415 AD. Researchers found the mention of Doctor Gennadius, a dreamer, in a letter written by Saint Augustine that talks about lucid dreaming.

Sir Thomas Browne, a famous physician, and philosopher also did his best to understand dreams since they fascinated him. He also tried the technique of lucid dreaming and penned down his learnings in the book Religio Medici. He stated that "...yet in one dream I can compose a whole Comedy, behold the action, apprehend the jests and laugh myself awake at the conceits thereof."

Another famous philosopher, Samuel Pepys, wrote in his dream diary, "I had my Lady Castlemayne in my arms and was admitted to use all the dalliance I desired with her and then dreamt that this could not be awake, but that it was only a dream."

Marie-Jean-Léon, the Marquis d'Hervey de Saint Denys, published his book, "Les Rêves et Les Moyens de Les Diriger, Observations Pratiques ('Dreams and the ways to direct them; practical observations')" anonymously. It was in this book that he described the technique and also how he felt when he employed this technique in his dreams. He also stated that people could wake up in their dreams and learn to change the way they respond to various situations in the dream. He was known as the father of lucid dreaming.

Frederik (Willem) van Eeden, a Dutch writer and psychiatrist, wrote an article, "A Study of Dreams," wherein he talked about lucid dreaming; it was in this article that he coined this term. Some psychologists consider "lucid dreaming" a misnomer, since they believe van Eeden was talking about something different from a lucid

dream. Judging from his other works, van Eeden wante
have more control over their dreams, and therefore he us
"lucid".

Benefits of Lucid Dreaming

Now that you know what lucid dreaming is, let us look at some
benefits of this technique.

You Become More Aware

According to the Merriam Webster dictionary, lucidity is being
more aware. It is only when you extend awareness into your dream
state that you become aware of every event or situation taking place in
your dream. It is important to understand that this awareness is only a
reflection of your sensitivity to the various memories and thoughts in
your mind. When you are aware of what happens in your dreams, you
become aware of the different information stored in your brain. Lucid
dreaming is a technique where you manifest your awareness in both
your subconscious and conscious minds. There is a lot that you can
improve when you are more aware of this information.

Most people are lost in their emotions and thoughts throughout
the day, and they tend to act based on them. This is exactly what
happens when you are lost in a dream. When you are lucid during a
dream, you begin to focus on various aspects of your dream and relate
them to the thoughts and emotions stored in your subconscious mind.
This is a significant shift in your thought process since you no longer
react to a situation based on your emotions or thoughts but relate to
them directly because of your cognition.

You Are In Better Control

When you are aware of everything that happens in your mind, you
do not succumb to your emotions and thoughts. This technique is not
only about controlling everything that happens in your dream, but it
actually is about learning to control how you respond to various

situations. When you have this control, you can control your responses and react responsibly to your thoughts and emotions. You no longer react instantly to any situation but can focus on various aspects of the situation before you respond to them. This is a better way for you to deal with challenging situations in life.

Preventing Nightmares

When you use this technique during a nightmare, you can tell yourself that it is only a bad dream and not something happening in reality. You can also change the dream, so that it is no longer a nightmare. If you are unable to do the latter, you can challenge yourself and change the way you relate to the various situations happening in the dream. You can only do this since you know the dream is not real.

You Become More Creative

When you have lucid dreams, you can control how the dream progresses. When you are more aware of a dream, you can look for different ways to change the dream. This helps to explore how powerful your mind is and how you can use it to help you change your situation. If a dog is chasing you in your dream, you can change it to a puppy. You can also change the situation where the dog is no longer chasing you but only sniffing you, and you can pet him.

Lucid dreaming helps you change the way you think. You can take what you learn from your lucid dreams and apply it to your everyday life. You soon learn how to change negative emotions or thoughts into good ones. You can also learn to change your mood, so you are more cheerful and happy since you finally know that you create your experiences.

You Have Powerful Choices

When you have lucid dreams, you learn that you have a choice about how you want to deal with your thoughts and emotions. You can choose to witness your dreams, where you let the dream unfold but do not change any aspect of it, or you can change some parts of it.

The former is like watching a film, while the latter allows you to change the ending of the film. Regardless of what you choose to do, you will learn that you have a choice. Once you know this, you know you can choose how to respond to various situations. Do you find yourself getting mad at someone at work or at home? Well, you are choosing to feel that. You can change the way you respond to the situation, change the way you relate to things, control your thoughts and emotions, and finally control your life.

Through lucid dreaming, you can determine the way you work with your emotions and thoughts. This technique helps you understand that you constantly work with your mind. You can change the way you respond to various situations in your life when you learn to work with similar situations in your dreams. You can use the insights or learnings from lucid dreaming, applying them to everyday situations in your life. It is only when you learn to focus on your dreams that you learn to be in a more awake state in life.

Chapter Three: Lucid Dreaming and Astral Projection

Most people tend to use astral production and lucid dreaming interchangeably since they believe they are the same thing. It is important to understand that these two are completely different phenomena or experiences. The most important difference between the two is that lucid dreaming only happens in a dream, while astral projection happens in the astral world, which is a dimension that is not a part of the physical world. Another difference to note is that astral projection is considered to be a real experience while lucid dreaming is not. The latter is only a phenomenon where you are more aware of what is happening in the dream, while the former is where the person experiences his consciousness in the astral realm.

When you try astral projection, you separate your consciousness from your physical body. Your consciousness then travels to a different plane where your astral body resides. It is never easy to do something like this, and it is for this reason most practitioners use specific beats, known as binaural beats, to help them ease into this projection.

What you must understand is that there is already an astral plane. Your consciousness is only visiting that plane, and thus, you cannot change or manipulate anything in that environment. You can also not change the way other people react or behave in that plane. Most people believe that astral projections are similar to near-death experiences since your soul leaves the body to move to a different dimension. People who practice astral projection often find themselves looking down at their physical bodies. Some people experience this phenomenon when they find themselves in near-death situations.

If you want to understand these experiences better, it is important to learn the fundamental differences between the phenomena.

In lucid dreaming,

- You only experience a dream
- You are not conscious
- You can be wherever you want to be (for example, the ocean, your childhood home, desert, etc.)
- You can change everything in your dream, including the characters and the environment
- Your soul or consciousness does not leave the body
- At the end of the experience, you find yourself awake

In astral projection,

- You are wide awake, and you separate or project your soul from your physical body
- The experience starts where you are currently (for example, your bedroom, office, living room, the park, etc.)
- Your body no longer has a consciousness since you have separated it from the body
- You can never change the way other people or inhabitants in the astral plane react to a situation
- It is easy to manipulate certain parts of this environment
- When you want to finish or end the astral projection, your consciousness returns to the physical body

Is Lucid Dreaming Necessary for Astral Projection?

You do not have to learn the technique of lucid dreaming if you want to project your consciousness from your physical body. You can learn how to project your consciousness from your body without learning how to maintain lucidity in a dream. Many people can separate their consciousness from their body by simply laying down on their bed. When you learn astral projection, you can project your consciousness from your body in the movie theater, at a restaurant, or even when you are at work. That being said, if you can maintain lucidity in a dream, it becomes easier for you to learn how to project your consciousness.

As mentioned earlier, some people can project their consciousness by simply lying down on the bed and closing their eyes. Others may have done this without realizing that they are projecting their consciousness out of their body, and they may be afraid that they have died. They may stand next to their body and wonder what happened to them. This is a strange situation to be in, but you can force your consciousness to move back into your body. The fear of death will naturally incline you do this.

Using Lucid Dreaming to Start Astral Projection

It is very difficult to master the art of lucid dreaming. If you want to maintain awareness or lucidity in a dream, you must ensure that you make your mind up even when you are asleep. This is something you must develop if you want to consciously project your consciousness into the astral plane. If you want to separate your consciousness from your physical body, you must learn how to move your consciousness or push it out from your physical body. It is only when you push it out that you can move it into the astral vehicle, which is also known as the astral body. When you separate your consciousness from your physical body, you push it into your astral or ghostly body. When you master lucid dreaming, you learn to keep your mind active and aware even when your body is sleeping.

What is Astral Projection?

The easiest way to separate your consciousness from your physical body is to learn how lucid dreaming works. This book will help you learn various aspects of lucid dreaming and what you can do to ease into it. Once you master this technique, use this as the foundation to help with astral projection. When you begin to focus on astral projection during lucid dreaming, you may find yourself paralyzed for a few seconds or minutes when you wake up. Your body only does this to protect you in your waking life, and help your mind determine whether you are in a dream or in a waking state. When your body is in this state, you should try to stretch or push your astral body away from your physical body. When you do this, you will feel like your consciousness or soul is moving away from your body. Do not be afraid when this happens, since this is how your body should react.

Let us understand astral projection using an analogy. During winter, you leave home wearing multiple layers of clothing and thermals that cling to your body for warmth. When you come back home, you remove layers of clothes and finally stretch out of the thermals. When you try astral projection, you notice that your consciousness is trying to stretch away from your physical body, much like the thermals.

Many people believe it is easy for them to cast their awareness or consciousness out of their bodies. They think they can have dual consciousness, and simply get out or move out of their physical body, but this is not what happens. If you successfully project your soul or consciousness from your physical body and look back at where you were a few moments ago, you see that your body is still on the couch or bed. You do not feel like you are still lying down, or that you are in a dream. You are finally awake and are standing next to your bed.

When you find yourself in this situation, you cannot feel your head on the pillow. You only see your body in that position. If someone were to tug or pull your arm, you could feel this even when you have projected your consciousness from your body. Your body has a cord that connects it to your soul or astral projection, and it uses this to ensure you return safely to your body. Your body will want to pull your consciousness or soul back into it quickly when you go astral the first few times.

When you go astral, try to push your soul as far away from your body as you can, so that your body cannot tug the soul back to it. If you are ready to go back into your body, you should only focus on that thought, and your body will tug the soul back into it. If you find yourself in terrible situations, you can use the help of spirits to guide you back into your body.

Some Things You Need to Know

There are times when you have may have a lucid dream, followed by a sense or feeling that you are separating your consciousness from your physical body. You must understand that this is not an astral projection. This is only a dream. If George Clooney or Julia Roberts is in your astral projection, you must remember you are dreaming. There are times when you may not fully move out of your body even when you have an astral projection, and this can be very frustrating. If your thoughts are not strong enough, and you cannot focus on pushing your consciousness from your body, you may move very quickly into a lucid dream. This is not an astral projection, even though it may be a great experience.

Some people feel they have experienced astral projection but not by leaving their bodies. What happens is that you can make your body vibrate at a different frequency that makes it easier for you to feel the astral plane, but your astral body does not stretch. This may have happened to many people who tried astral projection. You are in the astral plane, but your consciousness is not going anywhere; it is plugged into your physical body. When you do this, you may attract some negative emotions, entities, or thoughts that will suck your energy away, and this is something you do not want.

In other cases, you may find it easy to separate your soul or astral body from your physical body, taking the help of some energies or entities. If you know someone who can project his soul or consciousness from his body, ask him to help you through the process. It is a very tricky technique, and you need to have some training or help.

Chapter Four: Lucid Dreaming and Shamanic Journeying

The definitions of shamanic journeying and lucid dreaming vary depending on culture, and sometimes on resistance based on personal experiences. As you read earlier, the concepts and techniques of lucid dreaming came into existence thousands of years ago. Many indigenous cultures still use the concept of lucid dreaming as a form of therapy and practice it regularly. Experts believe that lucid dreaming is a form of shamanic therapy, a method used by soothsayers, healers, and medicine men to access energies, information, and insight. This means that lucid dreaming is not a fundamental concept by itself, but the technology or foundation of various shamanic methods.

The Conquerors of Consciousness

This is extremely different from how people today learn about lucid dreaming. People are now told that lucid dreaming is only a technique used when they want to indulge their fantasies, seek pleasure, or entertain themselves. There is nothing wrong with this definition of lucid dreaming, but this is a very limited definition. Many companies that manufacture lucid dreaming machines often use this definition to attract customers to boost their sales. They tell people they can seek pleasure through lucid dreaming, and this makes people purchase those machines to satiate their cravings.

It is unfortunate that people believe they can achieve whatever they want in their dreams, since it is only a dream, after all. The objective of any business working in this industry is to tap the ego of the buyer. According to Western civilization, it is our noble right to seize everything we want, because our desires matter the most. People are selfish, and when they fantasize about their dreams, they find a way to soothe their egos. They use their dreams to achieve everything they want but cannot achieve in real life.

Many people believe that a dream is a forest waiting to be plundered. Those who believe that their dreams have some meaning find it easier to use that meaning in their waking life. Sigmund Freud believed that people used dream interpretation only to satisfy or soothe their ego. Carl Jung, however, stated that people could drill into their subconscious mind during their dreams, even though this can hurt their conscious mind.

The objective of a lucid dreaming technique is to explore your dream, manipulate or change the dream, and conquer your thoughts and emotions. Lucid dreaming places you, the dreamer, at the center of your dream. Since you are the creator of your landscape, you can change everything about it. You conquer your consciousness and strike a balance between your subconscious and conscious minds.

The Negative Effects of Lucid Dreaming

The movie "The Men Who Stare at Goats" loosely represents some of the principles we have discussed, portraying a scenario in which the U.S. military tried to develop psi-based remote viewing to identify or detect targets. The movie "Inception" portrays a scenario in which the military assigned a task force to identify locations, targets, and people using lucid dreaming.

All of this work was once classified but is now available in the US Military database. It was in 1995 that the U.S. military decided there was no way remote viewing could be used to achieve the best results. Various programs, such as Gondala Wish, Sunstreak, and Stargate, did have some success with remote viewing. Dale Graff, the previous chief of Stargate, explained the process in his book "Tracks in the Psychic Wilderness," and mentioned how the team located a Russian airplane using remote viewing.

This means you need to be consistent with your practice if you want to maintain lucidity when you dream. You need to have an active imagination, but do not have to work with any higher power or energy. Shamanism is a different practice since the healers and medicine men use different energies and powers to compete with each other. They also use different spells and herbs. Lucid dreaming is not very different from Shamanism. Robert Waggoner, a psychotherapist, pointed out that one can use lucid dreaming to intrude into others' dreams, and no machine or tool is needed to do this.

The Emergence of Spirituality

Most people believe lucid dreams are used to stabilize the dreamer's hold on the dream. Lucid dreams, however, can also destabilize the dreamer's hold, and there are times when the dream can open doors to other worlds. You cannot prevent a nightmare from being uncontrollably bad, even if you maintain lucidity during your dream. When you confront these dark spirits and focus on your unconscious mind, you can unleash your spirituality. The American Psychiatric Association has listed spiritual emergence as a diagnostic category and claims it can lead to both spiritual and existential distress if not monitored correctly. You may have such dreams when you are under stress or duress, and also when you are unsure of where life will take you when you move from one role to another. Scott Sparrow, a psychotherapist, stated that the fear some people experience when they have lucid dreams helps them control their dreams, and therefore it is a necessary adversary.

Many people have had terrible cramping and other physical ailments after they practice lucid dreaming. Metaphorically, you can say that these people had trouble digesting their lucid dreams, and therefore felt pain. Ken Kelzer, a psychotherapist and lucid dreamer, also talks about his negative psychological and physical symptoms after lucid dreaming. He detailed his experiences in his book, "The Sun and the Shadow." If you are serious about lucid dreaming, you should do your best to ensure you create the right setting and environment for your dream sessions.

Ask yourself the following questions:

- Is the space I am working in safe for this practice?
- Is there a specific time when I should practice lucid dreaming?
- Can I ask someone to help me through this practice?

How to Initiate Yourself

By now, you may have gathered that lucid dreaming is not easy, and when you let yourself become aware that you are in a dream, you must learn to strike a balance between the control you can exercise and your awareness. This is the only way you can truly meet the various forces and entities in the spirit realm. It is best to look at your dream like a private initiation.

Some people also have terrible dreams wherein they find themselves lucid. They may dream about death, pain, and sorrow, and may see dead bodies, demons, ghosts, or fire. These are analogous to different initiation dreams that people have when they practice shamanic rituals. Ethnographers believe that these dreams help an individual express his essence and helps the person connect with various other energies in the world. The following is an example of a lucid dream taken from the book, "Sleep Paralysis: A Dreamer's Guide."

"I was reading when I noticed that the wall (about 6 feet from the end of my bed) started to sort of wobble. My body was paralyzed, unable to move. My breathing was kind of non-existent, though I desperately needed more air. Suddenly, it opened up into a black void, like a 9 feet black hole, vaguely the shape of a figure. "O my God," I thought, "I am dreaming. This can't be true." The black hole oozed into the room. I was beyond terror. I still don't understand how my heart didn't collapse. The blackness started molding itself into a recognizable shape. It became a 9 ft tall Japanese devil or devilish-looking Samurai. Viciously grinning, he said, "You are not dreaming. You thought you could 'integrate me.'" He then, in one sweeping movement, stretched out his enormous black hand, grabbed me, stuffed me into his blood-red mouth, and swallowed me. Then I fell into unconsciousness for a moment; now, a vortex pulled me down into an abyss of no dimensions. All of a sudden, I was spat back out into his hand. Somehow, I had crystallized into a red ruby. I WAS a ruby; I felt like a ruby. So, there I was, in the big hand of a giant, looking at him, and he is looking at me. In that moment of seeing each other, something happened. We looked at each other, became truly aware of each other, and then, there was love. I know what the mystics talk about/can't talk about. There is believing, and then, there is knowing."

If you read the initiation dream carefully, you know the demon in the dream scoffed at the individual's paradigm. James Hillman, a depth psychologist, suggested that your dream figure is not only a representation of who you are. It is a representation of your entire being. In the above dream, the dreamer surrendered herself to the demon and died. She fell into an abyss and was reborn with a new understanding of life.

The Revolution of Lucid Dreaming

People often use dream control as a means to surrender. This helps them learn to live in the present and go with the flow. Most people use the tension between working with the unknown and maintaining awareness in a dream to help them connect to their subconscious mind. This helps them maintain lucidity for longer periods in their dreams. It is of utmost importance now for dreamers to tap into the energy and wisdom of our ancestors to understand various events taking place in the world. This wisdom can help us understand our communities better and help us assess the effects of the economy on the environment and civilization.

Lee Irwin, a famous anthropologist, talked about how waking visions and big dreams integrated with opposing worldviews and conflicting paradigms during the clash between the West and the Native Americans in the seventeenth, eighteenth, and nineteenth centuries. This clash led to the rise of leaders who were both healers and visionaries who could lead forces against the colonial West. Barbara Tedlock, an anthropologist, talked about the effect of dreams on the Mayan civilization during the civil war in Guatemala in the 1980s. People within these communities were led by dreamers and visionaries who found a way to preserve their traditions while they accepted new cultures. These communities participated in the economy while they continued to follow their culture and faith.

That being said, you cannot succeed only because you have a dream. You can use the power of these dreams to help you create a template, making it easier for you to survive against all the odds. People now know their limitations in the current world, but they are still unaware of the destructive power of the world. We can use the power of dreams to prevent destruction, but to do this, we must be open to remembering them, sharing them with the world, and acting upon our dreams with hearts and eyes wide open.

Chapter Five: Preparation for Learning Lucid Dreaming

Most beginners have many questions about lucid dreaming, and this chapter answers some of those questions. You can use the information in this chapter to prepare yourself for a lucid dreaming experience.

When can I have my first lucid dream?

Experts believe that beginners can have their first lucid dream anywhere between three and thirty days from starting a lucid-dreaming program. This is dependent on their focus and how well they follow all the instructions to help them practice mindfulness. This book is only a guide, and there are some people who already have the necessary skills to help them become aware of their dream on their first attempt. Some may take months or years to develop this skill, and if you are not fully committed to it, you may take longer. Ask yourself the following questions if you are unable to have your first lucid dream:

- Do I spend enough time every morning to write down my dreams?
- Do I meditate for at least ten minutes every day?

- Am I doing everything in my power to improve my self-awareness every day?
- Do I perform enough reality checks each day? How frequently do I perform these checks?
- Did I develop a plan for what I want to do in my first lucid dream?
- Am I planting various ideas for my lucid dream in my subconscious mind?
- Have I learned the right techniques?

Can lucid dreams harm me?

You are not going to be in any physical danger, but you should be prepared to feel differently. You also need to ensure you are open to having new experiences. None of these experiences can hurt you, but you may find some of them a little odd.

Can I switch to a lucid state as a beginner?

Practice makes perfect, but most people experience a lucid dream in a few nights. You can use different techniques given in the book to help you maintain lucidity in your dream.

Can I have nightmares in a lucid state?

You can have a good or bad dream when you sleep, and you can be lucid in either of those dreams. The only difference is that you may be in an unpleasant dream. If you maintain lucidity, you can play an active role in controlling this situation, as you have a clear understanding of the situation you are in. It is only when you do this that you can confront the thoughts and images giving you this nightmare.

Are there signs to help me know I'm lucid?

If you use dreams to initiate lucid dreaming, you become aware or lucid when you know you are dreaming. If you have watched movies, you know that some characters realize they are dreaming, but they do not know how to control various aspects of that dream. They may scream or jerk awake, and may not even remember what they were dreaming about. You must understand that this is not lucid dreaming.

Lucid dreaming has very different effects on your life. When you are aware that you are dreaming and you say that out loud, a certain clarity of thought rushes into your mind. You begin to focus on every aspect of your dream and are more aware of your body. Lucid dreaming is much like a waking experience, and it is only when you feel this way that you can take in a lot of information from your surroundings.

Your dreams often have different features, and it is easy for these features to change even when you have lucid dreams. For example, you may be playing with puppies, and these puppies can change into boxes or clothes. You can, however, go back to playing with puppies if you maintain lucidity. These subtle changes cannot be controlled even when you remain lucid during a dream. Your subconscious mind plays an important role in this.

Can I remain lucid for longer?

Most lucid dreamers, especially beginners, cannot control the length of their lucid dreams. They may be too excited in their dream, and this wakes their physical body. There are times when you may forget you are lucid in a dream, and your subconscious mind may take control over everything in your dream. When this happens, it becomes a regular dream since you no longer have control. If you want to dream for longer, you should learn to stay focused and calm when you dream. You should learn to stay grounded mentally and tell yourself that you are only dreaming.

One of the easiest ways to stay lucid in your dreams for longer is to perform reality checks. You can either say, "I am dreaming", out loud, or walk around. This energy will stimulate your mind and keep it active. You can also make your conscious mind focus on your dream body and avoid looking at your physical body. If you follow these techniques, you can experience a lucid dream for as long as 60 minutes.

Can I add more elements and colors to the scenery?

It is difficult, especially if you are a beginner, for you to change the dream scene. One of the main reasons why this happens is that you don't think this can happen in your dream. Since you are a beginner, you do not understand how to control your dreams, which makes it hard for you to change anything about your dream.

The best way to help you understand the limits of your control is to work with your subconscious mind to understand your dream's logic. You can do the following to change some aspects of the scenery:

- Walk around in your dream and find the door. Visualize that you will move to a different world when you walk through this door.
- If you have lakes or other water bodies in your scenery, think about them as portals and jump in.
- You can also use a mirror portal to move from your current dream world into another.
- If you are watching a movie or TV series, change the scene and jump into it. You will see the world around you become 3-dimensional.
- Look away from the current dream scene and imagine a change in the scene. When you finally turn around, you will see a whole new world.

There are many things you can do if the only trouble is creativity. You must remember that your consciousness plays a significant role when it comes to your dreams. If you are unsure of your strengths and constantly wonder if you can change the different aspects of your dreams, your confidence may falter. If you learn from your mistakes and experiences and remain confident, you will learn there are many things you can do when you dream.

Can I dream that I am flying?

Most people want to learn how to fly when they have lucid dreams. They often want to master this art before they do anything else. Having said that, if you are new to lucid dreaming, you must avoid this since the concept is slightly difficult to grasp. Some people are lucky, and they take off like Superman while there are others who may bump into buildings, some who cannot get off the ground because of gravity, and others who get stuck on clotheslines.

Let us take the example of the movie "The Matrix". When Neo and Morpheus fight in the virtual world, the former beat the latter easily. Why do you think Neo was better? Was it because he was smarter, fitter, or stronger? No, all it took him was a little confidence. He believed he was better than Morpheus, and this belief helped him win the fight.

The same idea works with lucid dreams as well. You need to learn the art of flying when you have lucid dreams. This makes it easier for you to fly when you master maintaining lucidity in later dreams.

Can lucid dreams cause fatigue?

This is another myth. People dream during their REM sleep, and they may dream for over ninety minutes. An experienced lucid dreamer may have at least three lucid dreams in a week, and each dream may last for at least fifteen minutes. Some people believe this is like lost sleep because their mind is not quite at rest, but this is not too much time at all. Lucid dreams can give you a natural high, which leaves you with extra energy throughout the day. Some people experience lucid dreaming every night, in each of their sleep cycles. This means a lucid dream is not restricted only to their REM sleep. They have only had lucid dreams, and they have never complained about their lack of energy.

Some people choose to have normal dreams, and they let go of their lucidity when they have nothing else to add to their dream. There are others who choose to snap out of their lucid state. They wake up and open their eyes before they go back to bed. A very small number of people have had trouble with their dreams and are unable to sleep without any disturbances. This does make them feel a little sleep deprived throughout the day.

If you experience lucid dreaming naturally, but are afraid of the intensity of your dreams, visit a doctor or specialist. You must remember that anything in excess is bad for your body and mind, and there is a way to snap out of lucidity.

Can I be stuck in the dreamscape?

Do you think you can get stuck in a lucid dream the same way a child may get hung up on a painting or horror movie? If this is the case, remember it is not possible, since it is only a dream and not your reality. You cannot get stuck in a lucid dream, much like how you cannot get stuck in a nightmare or a regular dream. Only movies use this as a plot. When you are lucid dreaming, you can choose to wake up when you desire. Most people begin lucid dreaming when they use it as a means to wake up from bad dreams or nightmares. They can close their dream eyes and yell at their mind to wake up. You can also use these moments to help you switch to a guided dream from a nightmare. It is possible for you to become engrossed in a false awakening state or lucid nightmare. This is, however, not like being trapped forever in a dream. These states are both enlightening and frightening, and they have the same length as your REM sleep.

Do my dreams represent my psychic abilities?

Most people are under the misconception that their dreams represent their underlying psychic abilities. What is most important to understand is that nothing becomes real, simply because you want it to. If this were the case, everybody would win $1,000,000 or look exactly how they want to. There is little or no research that shows that dreams have psychic capabilities. People have heard of a friend who may have had this amazing psychic dream, so there is a possibility that such dreams are real. You must bear in mind that some stories are fabricated, and there may be some coincidences.

Can I communicate with my subconscious?

It is important to remember that your dreams are memories, emotions, and thoughts taken from your subconscious mind. This means there is two-way communication between your subconscious and conscious minds. One of the easiest ways to do this is to communicate with yourself in the dream. You can ask yourself some questions to communicate with your subconscious. This helps you strengthen the connection between your subconscious and conscious minds.

Do I die in real life if I die in a lucid dream?

This is untrue, and research shows that lucid dreams do not have a direct impact on your body. You may be chased by a dog, hurt yourself, or even die in a lucid dream. There are times when you may have fallen from a tower or the topmost floor of a building. This does not mean you died in reality. When you wake up, you realize that it was a dream, and it obviously did not kill you.

Can I have false awakenings?

A false awakening is a situation where you still are asleep, but your body believes you are awake. This is a very different state of mind, and you may have some vivid experiences similar to lucid dreams. Some people get out of bed, get dressed, grab a quick breakfast, and ride to work even in their false awakening state. They can perform such actions since they are in autopilot mode. This means that the experience is not fun and cannot be controlled. Having said that, the realism is quite shocking, which is why most people do not realize when they are in a false awakening state.

Lucid dreamers often have more experiences with false awakening than other people, and this is due to a clash between their consciousness and the dream world. It is an odd side effect of lucid dreaming but is not dangerous. This phenomenon can also lead to the development of dreams in the waking state, known as conscious dreams. Many movies have used false awakenings as a part of the plot to help viewers understand the characters' fears. One of the easiest ways to identify a false awakening is to check whether you are in a dream state or reality.

Can I use machines?

There are many machines you can use to help you with lucid dreaming, such as REM Dreamer, DreamMask and NovaDreamer. These machines use various lucidity triggers, and your subconscious mind uses these triggers in your dream. It is your job to focus on these triggers or cues, to help you understand or become more aware of yourself in the dream. These machines do not ensure that you remain lucid during your dreams, but when you use them correctly, you can improve the chances of staying lucid. These machines can also shift your consciousness from your physical body into the dreamscape.

How do I use brainwave music or messages?

Brain wave music or messaging is one of the easiest ways to shift from the waking state to a meditative state. This entertainment uses precision audio technology which stimulates the brain to move into a deeply meditative, calm, and relaxed state. This form of entertainment is good for the following reasons:

- This entertainment helps you switch from the waking state to a meditative state immediately, and improves your visualization and self-awareness, thereby helping you stay conscious and aware of yourself in different states.
- This form of entertainment also helps you enter the BAMA, or Body Asleep/Mind Awake state, and this is one of the best ways to have a lucid dream. You can also have an out of body experience when you are in this state. When you are in this state, your mind works hard to ensure that your body is in the dream state and asleep.

Are dream herbs good?

You can use dream herbs at times if you want to improve the intensity of your dreams. Some herbs also help you recall your dreams better. There are times when you may have meaningful, vivid, and insightful dreams when you take dream herbs. Some experts recommend herbs if you want to create or have interesting experiences in your dreams. You can also experiment with them to learn more about your mind, how you react to dreams, and, sometimes, just for fun.

Can I induce out of body experiences (OBE) using lucid dreams?

We discussed out of body experiences, also known as astral projections, in the third chapter of the book. Lucid dreaming can induce an out of body experience. There are times when you may have unexplained or unimaginable experiences even when you practice lucid dreaming techniques. There may be times when you feel like your consciousness is exiting your body when you have a

---

lucid dream. This is probably only a transition your consciousness is making when it moves from your physical body to the dream or imaginary body. This experience is like a false awakening.

Chapter Six: Preparing for a Lucid Dream Experience

Most people wonder how quickly they can have lucid dreams, and what most people do not know is that you can have a lucid dream the day you read about it. You can have a lucid dream within the first few nights of your initial attempt, since the only thing you have to do focus on your dream reality. This means you must become aware of your dream, but this is easier said than done.

Some people are not as lucky, and some may even take a month before they experience a lucid dream. The timeline varies between individuals, but some people only need to focus in the right direction for them to have lucid dreams. Having said that, you should not worry if you are unable to have a lucid dream the night you finish reading this book. It may take you some time to prepare yourself mentally and physically before you have a lucid dream. When you use the various techniques mentioned in this book, you will know exactly what you need to do to have lucid dreams. There will come a day when you do not have to put in so much effort to have a lucid dream. All you will need to do is focus on a thought or picture while you go to sleep and know that you will dream about that at night.

This chapter focuses on some tips and strategies you can use to experience lucid dreams. Before we dive into these methods, let us establish your goals.

Understand Your Goals

You must do the following when you learn various lucid dreaming techniques.

- Increase your chances of recalling your dreams. Since you dream for at least 100 minutes every night, pay attention to everything happening in your dream.
- Make sure you focus on different aspects of your dreams, such as sounds, sensations, sights, and feelings.
- Focus on your thoughts and learn to recognize when you are dreaming. This means you must learn to differentiate between dreams and reality. You can do this easily using reality checks, and we will cover these in detail in this chapter.
- Learn to become more aware of your life, so you become more aware of your dreams.
- Push your mind into becoming more aware when you have dreams. This is the only way you can have more lucid dreams.
- Learn visualization skills to help you manifest your dream. You can also visualize being in a lucid dream.
- Learn to focus on the content of your dream before you go to bed. We will look at this technique in detail later in the chapter.

When you incorporate the objectives mentioned above in your life, you can have lucid dreams every night. You must understand that your dreams only reflect the memories, thoughts, emotions, and experiences you have during your waking life. It is for this reason you can have a lucid dream by just thinking about something that transpired during the day.

Tips and Techniques

Learn

When you want to develop a skill, you must learn everything about that skill. This book has all the information you need about lucid dreaming, but there are tons of articles and videos out there to help you further in your journey.

Use Checks

I am sure you know what a reality check is. You should perform at least two dozen reality checks every day, especially at the beginning. You can decrease the number of reality checks you perform as you improve and develop your skills. These reality checks do not take more than a few seconds to perform. Consider the following example:

- Look at your hands.
- If there is a wall next to you, try to push your palms through the wall.
- If you are in a dream, your hand will go through the wall, but if you are not, your palms touch the surface of the wall.

The objective of a reality check is to help you determine whether you are asleep or awake. The outcome of any activity you perform will be different depending on your state. When you repeat such an action numerous times every day, it becomes muscle memory. Therefore, when you are dreaming, you can either perform the same reality check or use any other technique to determine if you are in a dream. This will help activate the part of your mind that focuses on various aspects of the dream, thereby inducing lucidity.

Reduce Screen Time

You should turn off every device, such as mobile phones, laptops, tablets, televisions, Kindles, etc., at least an hour before you go to bed. Turn off all the lights in your room, so you encourage your body and mind to go to sleep. This is the only way your brain releases enough melatonin to force your body to go to sleep. Keep your environment dark since light affects the production of melatonin.

Use Alarms

Most beginners get this step wrong when they start learning about lucid dreaming. If you follow the steps mentioned in this section carefully, you can improve. You should set the alarm to go off at least five hours after you go to bed. The objective is to bring you out of your REM sleep. You will, however, go right back to sleep using the methods mentioned in the next few steps and return to a state of lucid dreaming. If you want to succeed at using this method, keep the following points in mind:

- Keep your eyes shut when you try to turn off the alarm. Make sure your phone or clock is close to you, so you can reach it without having to open your eyes.
- Do not use a blaring sound as the alarm. Yes, the alarm should wake you up, but when you use buzzing sounds, your mind and body become active, making it difficult for you to go back to a state of lucid dreaming. Therefore, use something pleasant as the alarm.

Do Not Open Your Eyes

It is extremely important to do this, especially when you wake up from a dream. You must keep your eyes closed, so you convince your body to go back to sleep. Your mind, however, should be slightly awake.

Use WBTB

Wake Back to Bed, or WBTB is a method you use to train your body to go back to sleep even when your mind is alert. There may be times when you suddenly wake from sleep. It is during those times that you should learn to go back to sleep while your mind is still active, making it easier for you to maintain lucidity when you have a dream. This may sound impossible, but you can master this if you practice enough. We will look at this method in detail later in the book.

Meditate

In the previous sections, we looked at how important it is for you to separate your body and mind. If you practice meditation correctly, you can develop these skills. Buddhist monks are the best example here. They can meditate for as long as ten hours without taking a break. They forget about hunger and are not bothered by noises around them. They sit still, meaning they do not move even one muscle in their body. They are, however, looking at beautiful visions and experiencing everything that happens around them differently. You may wonder how you can achieve something as brilliant as this. They can do this since they have separated their mind from their body. Their bodies are in a position and state of rest, while their mind is active. Since lucid dreaming is similar to this, you must develop the same skill set.

Use Musical Aids

Many people use aids such as binaural beats and white noise to focus, concentrate, or sleep. These aids also help you when you want to experience lucid dreaming. The different frequencies being played in these musical aids always enter your ears at the same time. Your brain, however, still looks at these beats or music as a single frequency making it easier for you to focus or concentrate. There are numerous videos on YouTube with these tracks, or you can download an app that has a variety of music. If you want to use these for lucid dreaming, you must ensure that the frequency of this music matches the frequency of the brain waves that help you become aware during your dream. Experts recommend that you stick to music between the frequency 4 Hertz – 8 Hertz.

Play Games

When you play games such as *Counter-Strike* or *Age of Empires*, you are in a completely different world. You can explore and learn more about every aspect of this universe. If you play games such as *Defense of the Ancients* or *Dungeons and Dragons*, you may take up a role. Sometimes, you may want to take a different path to your teammates, just to see what's there. This is what you must do when you sleep, too. When you find yourself in a different world, focus on various aspects of that world, and explore it. It becomes easier to do this in your dreams when you play video games in your waking life.

Take Galantamine

Most Alzheimer's patients are given this natural supplement to improve their memory and brain function. Galantamine is a plant-based substance found in plants such as spider lily and dandelions. The substance can be used orally. According to the study, "Exploring the Effects of Galantamine Paired with Meditation and Dream Reliving on Recalled Dreams: Toward an integrated protocol for lucid dream induction and nightmare resolution (2018)," this supplement improves the quality of sleep during your REM stage. It also lengthens your sleep, thereby making it easier for you to remember your dreams. The study also showed that people who took this supplement had a higher chance of experiencing a lucid dream than those who took placebos.

Take Supplements

Experts recommend that you take vitamin B6 supplements if you want to ease into lucid dreaming. There is limited research to determine the correlation between lucid dreaming and this vitamin, but according to the study, "Effects of Pyridoxine on Dreaming: A Preliminary Study (2002)," Vitamin B6 increases the serotonin levels in your body which makes your dreams more colorful. You may also have vivid dreams if you take these supplements, and this makes it easier to remember them the following morning.

Time

You must understand that it will take time for you to learn a new skill. Therefore, give yourself enough time to do the following:
- Maintain a journal wherein you write your dreams
- Meditate and visualize the dream during the day
- Maintain a routine before you go to bed
- Learn more about lucid dreaming
- Prepare yourself for bed

It is not recommended that you practice any lucid dreaming technique if you have a busy life. If you work every day or are a student, you have some time commitments that may make it hard for you to set some time out regularly to focus on these techniques. You should ideally spend at least thirty minutes every day to develop the necessary skills. Therefore, plan your day in advance, so you have sufficient time to practice lucid dreaming techniques.

Discipline

You must maintain a disciplined approach if you want to learn how to remain lucid when you dream, which is a little like learning a new sport or technical skill. It is only when you practice that you become a better player or coder. You may not achieve the expected results when you attempt to maintain lucidity in your dreams for the first few times. You are only laying the foundation to help you become more aware of your dreams in the future. If you are committed to your routine and techniques, you can get the most out of lucid dreaming. Therefore, you must be disciplined in your approach. You should be consistent with the various tips and techniques you use for at least thirty days.

Passion

Was there some task at work that you hated doing? Did you put in as much effort to complete this task as you did to complete your favorite tasks? The point of these questions is to help you understand that passion is what makes learning more fun. It is only when you are passionate about something that you are motivated to stick to the training. This is the only way you can maintain lucidity during your dreams.

Tips to Ease into a Lucid Dream

It may be extremely fun to have a lucid dream, but it is a difficult journey. The experience can also be daunting. Having said that, when you have a lucid dream, you could change your life for the better. We have looked at some of the benefits of lucid dreaming earlier in the book.

This is a skill you must develop, and like every other skill, it does take some time for you to become aware of being in a dream. There is no single way to do this, and there are numerous methods one can employ when they try to maintain lucidity during dreaming. This section lists some methods to help you begin your journey.

- Use a dream journal regularly and make a note of at least one dream after you wake up if you can remember them.
- Meditate for ten minutes every day, so you become aware of your thoughts and emotions.
- Look for different signs in your dreams to help you become more aware or lucid when you have dreams with similar signs.
- Ask yourself if you are dreaming. You can also perform a physical action to help you determine if you are dreaming or not.
- You can either use a spray with a relaxing aroma or fill your pillow with essences to calm your mind.
- Take some lucid dreaming pills; you want to increase the intensity or vividness of your dreams.
- If you wake up or jerk away when you have a dream, use the wake- induced lucid dreaming method to help you go back to sleep and continue to be aware of your dream.
- Purchase a good mattress, especially if you want to sleep well.
- When you drift off to sleep, focus on your surroundings, and observe any hallucinations that you may be having.
- You can induce lucid dreams through smells using aromatherapy. This form of lucid dreaming is known as Smell Induced Lucid Dreams.
- Observe the posture that works best for you. Relax into that posture before you go to bed.
- Experiment with different lucid dream techniques. We will cover some of these in detail later in the book.
- Use a lucid dreaming application to control your thoughts and emotions when you go to bed. You can download this on your laptop or phone.

- Watch a video before you go to bed, preferably a lucid dreaming video, so you motivate or stimulate your mind to become aware during a dream. Alternatively, you can also listen to subliminal messages or lucid dreaming hypnosis sessions.
- Use dream herbs to have memorable and vivid dreams.
- You can increase the intensity of your dreams by eating cheese before you go to bed.
- If you have trouble sleeping, especially during your REM cycle, visit a doctor, and find a way to get rid of these issues.
- When you are aware of a dream, you can also ask the dream to help you stay lucid when you have other dreams. This will stimulate your brain to remain conscious during all dreams.
- Visualize or manifest a plot that you want to see in your dream. You can use lucid dream movies to help you do this.
- Give yourself some time every day to daydream. This helps you explore various fantasies and realities.
- You can use mnemonic induction to help you have lucid dreams. Use this technique right before you go to bed. We will look at this technique in detail in the next chapter.
- If you are not very good at remembering dreams the following morning, you can set the alarm during your REM cycle. When you wake up, and if you have had a dream, write it down in your journal before you go back to sleep. Alternatively, you can also wear a digital watch that beeps every 60 minutes. You can use this beep to remind yourself to perform a reality check in your dream.
- Read more about Yoga Nidra.
- If you fall asleep in various locations, encourage your subconscious to have false awakenings.

- You can also use different methods to have out of body experiences, like astral projection.
- You can move into a lucid dream through sleep paralysis.
- If counting makes you sleep, count backward as you become drowsy. Say, "I am dreaming," before you move to the next number in the sequence.
- You can sleep during your day, especially after a workout.
- Relax every weekend, and practice the techniques mentioned in the book. This approach helps you determine the technique that works best for you.
- Most people are afraid of lucid dreams because they think it may harm their consciousness. This, however, is not true. All you must remember is that lucidity or awareness is a positive and powerful tool you can use to grow.
- Sleep for at least eight hours every night.
- You can meditate before you go to sleep or while you are sleeping.
- Use lucid dreams technology if you can afford it.

You can use different methods to make it easier for you to practice lucid dreaming. If this is overwhelming, remember this is only an overview of the various methods you can use. If you want to begin lucid dreaming tonight, use the following methods to become more aware during a dream.

Perform a Reality Check

When you dream, you must determine if you are actually in a dream. You can either stomp your foot or pluck a flower depending on where you are in your dream.

Visualize the Dream

You can plan what happens in your lucid dream. Focus on your desire, close your eyes, and visualize that thought or desire. You can also visualize and focus on being aware of your dream.

Repeat Your Steps

If you wake up in the middle of the night, repeat all the steps you performed before you went to bed. This helps you fall asleep easily.

Make sure you do not forget these tips. These techniques may sound a little weird or strange, and there are times when you may wonder why you are following them. It is normal to feel this way. You may not always get the right results when you use these techniques. Having said that, it is only when you master your basics that you can move on to the advanced techniques. When you have a lucid dream, you finally learn to differentiate between dreams and reality.

Since you are a beginner, it is important for you to maintain a routine so your consciousness remains lucid or aware during a dream.

Maintaining a Routine

This section gives you a basic routine you can use to ease into a lucid dream.

Meditation

There are times during the day when you are in a half-sleep state, and during these states, you may either feel drowsy or calm. When you feel this way, lie down on your bed or a couch and relax. Let your thoughts and emotions drift. The only thing you need to focus on is to force your body to fall asleep while you are conscious. To do this, focus on the thin cord that connects your body to your consciousness, and use the cord to push your mind away from your body. This is not only a very relaxing exercise but also creates hypnagogic sensations. You may see geometric patterns, feel as if you are floating, or view some dream impressions. Meditation is a great way to improve your visualization and awareness skills.

Journaling

If you want to lucid dream frequently, maintain a dream journal. Make a note of your dreams when you wake up every morning. Spend at least five minutes every morning to write down every dream you had. This not only makes it easier for you to recall your dreams but also helps you maintain lucidity when you dream. This step is extremely important, and therefore, you should not ignore it.

Planting an Idea

In this step, you can plant an idea or thought in your subconscious mind so that you dream about the idea later. This is nothing like inception since the idea is yours. One of the easiest ways to plant an idea in your subconscious mind is to visualize or fantasize about the character or plot during the day. Consider the following example: when you watch a horror movie, you constantly think about the demon or ghost chasing you. You also visualize shapes and other objects in the darkness, which can give you nightmares. You can use daydreams and happy thoughts to have good dreams, in the same way. These daydreams and happy thoughts will feature in your dream if they are visceral. Alternatively, you can also use the concept of visualization and manifestation to convince your mind that you will get lucid dreams tonight. If you make this thought the last thought of your day, you will definitely have a lucid dream.

You have turned your alarm off, so now close your eyes and begin to focus on the dream; this is where the magic begins. When you focus on your dream, your body soon begins to drift off to sleep. It will, however, test whether your mind is still awake. Your body may tell your brain that you need to curl, scratch your nose, pull the covers over your head, etc. Do not do this. When you do not move, your body believes that you are asleep. It will release control, and your unconscious mind takes over. You see shapes, colors, images, and scenic views, and all of these come together to create shapes and images. These will all come together and take some shape. When you are aware of these images and shapes, you are finally aware of your dreams.

Things to Do When you Are Aware

Now that you know what a lucid dream is, you must learn what to do when you become aware or are lucid in your dream. If you do not know what you must do, you may become too excited and wake up from your dream. Use the following techniques to help you stabilize the dream when you become aware that you are in a dream:

- Look at yourself and observe your movements
- Walk around and focus on how your feet feel on the ground
- Say something out loud
- Rub your palms together
- Feel the sensation of every movement when you walk or spin around in your dream

You cannot stay lucid in a dream if you do not use the right techniques. The techniques mentioned above stimulate your mind, which makes it easier for you to change your dream into reality. If you stimulate your mind and stabilize your presence or awareness in the dream, you can make this dream last longer.

Things to do in Your Dream

Once you learn to stabilize your thoughts and emotions in a lucid dream, you should also learn to calmly explore everything in the environment. You should never make changes to the dream or any aspect of it too soon. Do not do something too fancy, like teleporting yourself to the top of the Eiffel Tower, when you find yourself aware for the first time in your dream. If you do this, you may become too excited, and this may jerk you awake. When you start off with lucid dreaming, it is best for you to walk or float around, look at the environment, and soak in every object and aspect of that environment. You must still remember that your dream is only your virtual reality, and this is both living and tangible. This is the only way you can continue lucid dreaming.

Chapter Seven: 5 Lucid Dreaming Techniques

People have used different techniques to have lucid dreams. This chapter covers some of the simplest techniques approved by psychologists.

Dream Induced Lucid Dream (DILD)

As mentioned earlier, a dream induced lucid dream is one where you realize that you have a dream inside another dream. This method is beginner-friendly and easy. Most people who want to try lucid dreaming use this technique. The most important thing to remember about lucid dreaming is that you must be aware of or lucid in your dream. Some common techniques of DILD are:

All Day Awareness of ADA

When you are fully aware of yourself throughout the day, you can easily distinguish between your dream and the real world. You can use the various techniques mentioned above (reality checks) to help you become more aware of your dreams.

Using Checks

Most people never think they are dreaming since their mind always believes they are awake. When you decide to perform regular reality checks, you become more aware of the dream world and the real world. Your dreams become more clear and vivid when you improve your awareness.

Self-Hypnosis

Self-hypnosis is a state where you are relaxed. This technique is more like programming your mind to have a lucid dream.

Dream Signs

As mentioned earlier, a sign in your dream can be a cue that helps you determine if you are in a dream or not. When you pay attention to these cues and signs, you begin to notice them a lot more. This helps you have more lucidity in your dreams.

CAT or Cycle Adjustment Technique

Daniel Love was the one who created this technique, and there are three steps you should follow when you use this technique.

Step One

Set the alarm to at least sixty minutes before the usual time you wake up. You should do this every day for at least two weeks to help your body clock reset, because you may not have a lucid dream when you start off with this technique.

Step Two

After the fourteenth day, you can go back to your previous schedule, but wake up earlier every other day. This means you should follow the sequence: early, normal, early, normal. When you go to bed, let your body know that you want to wake up earlier than normal, and make sure to perform enough checks to determine whether you are asleep or awake. You should prepare yourself for the early morning before you go to bed each night.

You can sleep in on days when you wake up at your usual time, but avoid sleeping in for longer, so you do not disrupt your new cycle.

Step Three

Your body finally learns to wake up early and will expect your mind to do this, too. Since the body is active, it stimulates your mind, which in turn helps your mind retain consciousness even when you dream. This increases the chances of being lucid in a dream, and you may have lucid dreams at least four times every week.

So, what do you think you should do when you wake up earlier than usual? You can do almost anything, but ensure you do not go back to sleep. Keep performing reality checks every day and do it as often as possible when you wake up earlier than usual. This helps you stimulate your mind and keep it active throughout the day. You can then go about normally throughout your day. It is only when you do more reality checks that your mind can differentiate between a dream and reality.

WBTB

WBTB is an acronym for 'Wake Back to Bed,' and this is a simple technique. This is another form of DILD. Most people combine this technique with the MILD technique since this is one of the best ways to enhance lucid dreaming. The following are the steps to follow to perform this technique:

- Set the alarm for five hours after you have gone to bed.
- Take an hour before you go to bed to read more about lucid dreaming. This sends the right signals to your brain and stimulates it to remain active throughout your dream.
- When the alarm rings, do not open your eyes but force your body to go back to sleep while your mind is still active. Alternatively, you can also walk around while you focus on your dream.

There are a few more things you need to know about this technique.

As mentioned earlier, you have vivid dreams or lucid dreams during your REM sleep stage. Your first REM sleep state occurs an hour after you fall asleep, and you have additional REM sleep states every ninety minutes after the first state. The objective of this technique is to wake up during your REM state and go back to sleep as soon as you can. You should also ensure that you go back to your dream and stay aware that you are in a dream. It is best to visit a sleep lab or have someone watch you when you sleep. This is the best way for you to time your phases. You should repeat this method until you know when you are in your REM state.

Get Extra Sleep During Your REM State

You should sleep for longer during your REM sleep state. You can get some extra sleep during your REM sleep, and one of the most effective ways to do this is to stick to a sleep schedule. You must also ensure you sleep for as long as you can, so you wake up feeling refreshed and relaxed. It may be difficult to manage this, considering that, in the next step, you must wake up a few times each night. If you cannot go back to sleep immediately, you should look for a different method to use. Do not attempt this technique more than twice a week.

Wake Up

If you sleep for eight hours every night, you should set the alarm so it goes off four or five hours after you fall asleep. You are definitely going to be in a REM sleep state during those hours, but you cannot always pinpoint when it starts. The REM phases may last longer in later phases, and you may have more lucid and vivid dreams.

Stay Awake for Some Time

When you wake up, you should wake up and write your dream down in your journal, if you were having one. You can either walk around or get yourself something to eat. The objective is to ensure you remain conscious, and your mind is both alert and active. Your body, however, is still asleep and filled with the right hormones. Experts say that you can stay awake for as long as 30 minutes before you find it difficult to maintain lucidity in your dreams.

Focus Only on the Dream

You should focus on your dream before you go to sleep. After you have walked around for a bit, close your eyes and go to bed. If you could remember the dream you were having, you should recall that dream before you go back to bed. Visualize that you are back in the dream, and this may take some time for it to happen. There is, however, a decent chance that you may have this dream again.

Look for Other Ways to Concentrate

If you find it difficult to focus on your dream when you try to go back to sleep, you should use different ways to concentrate on your dream. If you do not remember anything about your dream, you can focus on some small movements, like moving your fingers. You should repeat this movement until you fall asleep.

MILD

MILD is an acronym for 'Mnemonic Induction of Lucid Dreams,' and it is best to combine this technique with WBTB. You need to concentrate when you use this method to practice lucid dreaming.

In this technique, you use mantras or phrases to help you convince your mind to maintain lucidity in your dreams. You can repeat this mantra, 'I know I am dreaming,' before you go to bed. This is the easiest way to convince your mind that you are only in a dream. You can also spend some time during the day to visualize a possible dream. You can tell your mind that you want to fly in your dream. Repeat this vision to yourself until you are sure the thought has manifested itself in your mind, or until you fall asleep.

This can take time to master, but if you are struggling, try to convince yourself that you must wake up immediately after your dream. Alternatively, you can use the WBTB method to do this. When you are awake, try to remember your dream, and make a note of it in your journal. Before you go back to bed, focus on your dream, and visualize it. You should use this technique only after you have practiced lucid dreaming for some time.

Autosuggestion

Autosuggestion is a highly effective technique and has been used in scientific research. This technique includes hypnosis, so only use it if you are comfortable with hypnosis. You use a mantra similar to the one we used in the previous chapter. You should repeat to yourself that you would have a lucid dream. Repeat this mantra continuously so that you convince your mind that you will have a lucid dream. Do not force this thought into your mind, since it can change the way your mind perceives the idea of lucid dreaming.

You can also use this technique to help you recall your dreams. Instead of telling yourself you will be lucid dreaming tonight, tell your mind that you will remember your dreams the following morning. When you focus on this thought, you can remember the dream the following morning. This method may be effective, but it does not work for everybody. If you want to improve the chances of success, use meditation to calm your mind down.

Follow the steps given below to use this technique:

- You should repeat to yourself every minute you get some time that you will have a lucid dream. This is the only way you can convince your mind to remain active during a dream.
- You can use any mantra. Consider the following:
  o I will know I am dreaming
  o I will have a lucid dream tonight
  o I will definitely be aware of everything in my dream

Continue to repeat this mantra until you go to bed. You must ensure you remain focused and make sure you say the same phrase repeatedly. This is the only way you can let your mind know you will remain active or lucid in your dream.

This may sound extremely simple, but this technique works best if you remember to be consistent. The only thing you must remember is that you should never force it. Do not force the lucid dream or the thought of a lucid dream, but let your mind become aware or lucid in your dream.

WILD

The WILD Method is the Body Asleep and Mind Awake technique that we talked about earlier in the book. This technique makes it easy for you to enter a state of lucid dreaming directly. Follow the steps given below if you want to use this technique:

- The first thing you must do is to lie down on your bed and close your eyes. Alternatively, you can wake up after four hours of sleep. To do this, you should relax both mentally and physically.

o The best way to relax is to meditate. This is one of the easiest ways to switch from your waking state to your dream state.

o Make sure you do not move too much but relax.

- When you are relaxed and calm, focus on the darkness, and let your thoughts wander. You need to follow up on any thought or image that comes to your mind when you are in this state. This is known as hypnagogia. According to the Merriam Webster dictionary, "A hypnagogic hallucination is a vivid, dream-like sensation that an individual hears, sees, feels, or even smells. It occurs near the start of sleep." The only thing you must do is to relax and stay calm.

- Now, create your dream scene. When you let your thoughts carry you away, you can create the right scene for your characters and dream. Visualize your dream with as much detail as you can. Spend some time to look at the surroundings. This is the only way your awareness becomes higher.

- You are finally in the body asleep and mind awake state, where your body is asleep, but your mind is awake. When everything is finally in place, you will be dreaming. You move from a waking state to the dreaming state consciously.

Third Eye Method

The third eye method, also known as the Chakra method, is one of the common techniques beginners used to remain lucid or aware when they dream. If you use this technique, you must focus on your third eye chakra or the space between your eyebrows. You also need to follow a synchronized breathing pattern since it helps your mind relax. This makes it easier for you to become aware of your dreams. The third eye method is based on the WILD technique, and the only difference is this method uses meditation. Use this method before you try the wake-induced lucid dream method. Follow the steps given below to practice this technique:

- The first thing you should do is go to bed and lie down. The objective of this method is to ensure you focus only on the energy in your third eye chakra. So, take deep breaths and focus on your third eye.
- Now, slowly begin to focus on having lucid dreams. When you fall asleep, your mind remains active and focuses on having lucid dreams. This is similar to the WILD step, and you can easily switch from the waking state to your dream state.
- The last thing you need to do is to focus on your breathing. You should focus on every aspect of your dream, so you have a lucid dream that night.

Chapter Eight: How to Explore your Dreamland

There are countless possibilities and scenarios you can explore in a lucid dream. Lucid dreams are not governed by the general principles of time and space regulating the physical world. However, some people are unaware of what they should do or where to start once they are in a lucid dream. If you don't know what to do after you get there, it defeats the purpose of lucid dreaming altogether. To make the most of your lucid dream, here are some simple suggestions you can use.

Start Flying

Channel your inner superhero and start flying! This is perhaps one of the exciting things you can ever try in a lucid dream. However, don't start flying unless you have stabilized yourself in the lucid dream. If you do it too quickly, chances are you will wake up. If you have ever wondered what it would feel like to fly like a bird in the sky, now is the time to explore it. To start flying, visualize that powerful energy is blasting off your feet, working against the gravity force, and pushing you upward.

Try Acrobatics

Do you want to swing from one vine to another like Tarzan? Or maybe leap from one building to another like the graceful cat woman?

If yes, try acrobatics! You don't have to worry about physical injuries or fatally injuring yourself while you swing effortlessly like an acrobat. Jump from one high-rise building to another or even somersault to see how high you could go. Let your inner Cirque Du Soleil performer guide you.

Meet Celebs

Who wouldn't want to meet their favorite celebrities? Irrespective of whether it's a movie star or a football player, you can meet whoever you want in your dream world. All you need to do is merely visualize the person you wish to meet and believe they will be present somewhere in your dreamland. For instance, they could live on the street you have visualized, and you merely need to go to the specific house. After all, there are truly no limits when it comes to lucid dreaming, and there is no point in restricting or limiting yourself by the constraints of the regular world.

Try Teleportation

Anyone who has watched sci-fi movies is often intrigued by the idea of teleportation. Imagine how simple it would be to move from one place to another without lifting a finger. Instead, you will use the power of your mind. You don't have to travel physically, but all you need to do is think about a destination, and voila, you are there. If this idea fascinates you, there is no time like the present to start exploring it. Once you have induced yourself into a lucid dream, try teleportation. You can jump from one place to another, or even one world to another. It's quite easy; all you need to do is visualize the location you want to go to, and will it into existence. After you visualize the place, slowly start spinning, and believe you will reach the destination once you stop spinning.

Become A Movie Star

Why should you limit yourself to just meeting your favorite celebrities? You now have the power to become a movie star. If you want to be in a movie, you can create your own movie in the dreamland. You are the actor, director, producer, and scriptwriter. If there is a movie you love, you can try recreating it. If you want, you can also get other celebrities to star in this dream movie of yours. To truly experience the power of lucid dreaming, try to make your dreams as realistic as you possibly can. Visualize every little detail and experience all the feelings.

Dream Sex

If you have had sex before, it's quite easy to conjure all these feelings in your lucid dream. Lucid dream sex is quite thrilling, and it's one of the most incredible things you can experience. You should remember that if you are just getting started with lucid dreaming, save all the exciting things until later. Unless you learn to ground yourself in the lucid dream, any exciting activity you indulge in will merely wake you up. Therefore, first, concentrate on mastering the art of lucid dreaming before you dream about exciting things.

All in all, your mind is extremely powerful, and you need to keep in mind that you shouldn't keep visualizing the same person in all your lucid dreams. It can become difficult to distinguish between reality and memories of the dream world. You will learn more about things you shouldn't do in the dreamland in later chapters.

Thought Control

Wouldn't it be amazing and amusing if you could read minds? The ability to know what others are thinking is an exciting thought, and humans have been exploring this possibility for ages. You can look at someone and precisely know what they are thinking without any filters and feel what they are experiencing. If you want to do this, you can use thought control. Merely look at a fictional character in your lucid dream space and channel your consciousness from your body into the dream character to discern what they are feeling.

Shapeshifting

Why don't you try shapeshifting? You can transform yourself into any beast that walks the Earth. Maybe you can shapeshift into a cheetah and experience what it's like to be the fastest living being on Earth. Or perhaps you could transform yourself into the majestic blue whale. Maybe you could try transforming yourself into a fictional creature, such as the griffin or a dragon. Imagine what it would feel like to be a fire-breathing dragon soaring in the sky.

Move Away from Earth

Several scientific fiction movies have explored the idea of life on another planet. If any of these ideas have ever intrigued you, now is the time to test them. You have the power to move away from Earth and live on another planet. Why don't you try traveling to Mars or perhaps Jupiter? You have the freedom to fly wherever you want and visit any of the planets. If you want to get a little more creative, you can think about inventing your own planet!

Relive Memories

You probably have many fond memories that fill you with joy. With lucid dreaming, you get an opportunity to relive those memories. If there are any instances in your life where you wish you reacted differently or had a different response to the situation, try reliving them once more. When it comes to lucid dreaming, you have complete control over what you dream about and how the dream progresses.

Stand in Space

Do you want to feel like a cosmonaut out in the space? Well, now is your time to do this. If you want, you can also give yourself a bird's eye view of what the universe looks like. The world is certainly quite large, and it would look brilliant from space. Once you learn how to fly perfectly in your lucid dream, use this newfound superpower to travel upwards. Go through the stratosphere until you reach outer space.

Listening to Music

Anything you experience in the dream is more magnified than it actually is in reality. Therefore, even a small activity becomes more pronounced and profound. Something as simple as listening to music can be elevated and taken to the next level. If you want, you can organize a personal concert with your favorite singer or even listen to opera! In a vivid dream, if you listen to music, the overall effect is certainly amplified. All the emotions and small nuances of music we often miss in the real world are magnified in lucid dreams. Once you listen to music in your lucid dreams, it will truly change how you feel about it in the real world. Everything you experience in the dreamland will stay with you because you are conscious and aware of it all, even while dreaming.

Try Something New

Are you scared of stepping out of your comfort zone? If yes, trying something new in your lucid dream is a good idea. After all, a lucid dream helps create a safe environment to explore whatever you want without any worries. If you want to skydive, try doing it in a lucid dream. Even if you have never done it before, all the memories stuck in your mind from the videos you watched or the stories you heard can be replayed in the dream-like state.

Slow-Motion

We live in an incredibly hectic and busy world. Everyone seems to be in a rush and hurry to get somewhere or the other. As soon as you wake up in the morning, you need to get dressed and rush to work. Once work ends, you need to rush home. If you want to give yourself a break from all this rush, take a break and enter your dream world. You can live life in slow motion in lucid dreams. You have the power to slow down time and live life in slow motion. When you are extremely busy, it's highly unlikely you can notice the small things in life. For instance, you might not have the time to slow down and smell the roses. In a lucid dream, you have all the time you need to do all this. When you live life in slow motion, you can finally experience the beauty of sunrise and sunset, the chirping of birds, and the simple joys of nature.

Control Time

How wonderful would it be if you could control time? With lucid dreaming, you can revisit your past, explore the future, or connect with your present. Irrespective of what you want to do, you have the power to do it. You can slow time down and can control it, too. You can revisit a historical occurrence, rewrite history in your mind, or pay a quick visit to your future.

Opposite Sex

It is often said men are from Mars, and women are from Venus. Were you ever curious about what the opposite sex feels and thinks? Now is the time to understand what it would be like to live life as your opposite sex. You can do all this without expensive, painful, and complicated surgeries. Follow the same technique which was mentioned for teleportation. Visualize what you want to achieve, start spinning, and once you stop spinning, you would be transformed into your opposite sex. Do you remember the move, "Switch?" The lead character in the movie, an alpha male, is transformed into a woman. Well, you can try this too!

Explore Another Character

You can conjure up any character you want in your dream state and change into that character. In fact, you can transform yourself into any person you want to be. Why limit yourself to celebrities and famous people? You transform yourself into your best friend, partner, parent, or even an acquaintance at work. This is also a great way to understand how others think. You are literally placing yourself in someone else's shoes. If you have a tough time associating with others or are lacking in empathy, try this technique. You can safely explore your boundaries and those of others without any harm. Try to have conversations with this dream character or the person you are transformed into.

Another simple idea is to explore the mind of your dream characters. For instance, if you are out for drinks with your friends, imagine the scenario in your head. Try playing out what the other people would say while having a good time. This technique comes in handy while you are analyzing different relationships in your life. For instance, if you have doubts about whether a relationship is healthy or not, try doing this.

Survive An Apocalypse

Do you like watching movies about the apocalypse? Be it a zombie invasion, an alien attack, or maybe the end of the world, irrespective of what you like, you have a chance to experience all of it. Did you have fun watching a zombie movie? Imagine how much more fun it would be if you were actually a part of that movie? Another brilliant thing about this technique is you can use your other superpowers to defeat these zombies or monsters you have imagined. For instance, you can fly like Superman, channel your inner Hulk, or do anything else that you want to. However, while you do this, ensure the dream doesn't turn into a nightmare. Whenever things start getting scary, consciously regather your thoughts and change the script. After all, the purpose of a lucid dream is not to wake up in a cold sweat.

Find Your Spirit Guide

Perhaps one of the most interesting and brilliant things you can do while exploring a lucid dream is to find your spirit guide. Your spirit guide or guardian angel will keep you safe and help you find solutions to any problems you might be experiencing in life. At times, simply saying, "I want to find my spirit guide," does the trick. It is believed you need to ask the entity, "Are you my spirit guide?" thrice to confirm it is your spirit guide indeed and not a malevolent entity. You will learn more about this in the subsequent chapters. If the entity doesn't confirm it thrice, it is not your spirit guide. Don't forget this rule whenever you summon your spirit guide in the dream world.

Deal With Your Fears

Do you have any fears or phobias? Maybe you are scared of closed spaces or public speaking. Perhaps spiders or deep water scares you. Regardless of your fears, you can safely explore the cause of your fears in a lucid dream. Whenever you get overwhelmed or scared, you can end the dream or turn it into something pleasant.

Practice Real-Life Scenarios

Are there any real-life scenarios that intimidate or overwhelm you? Perhaps you were nervous about a big presentation at work, or a job interview. Or maybe you are scared about going on a date. Irrespective of what the circumstance is, you can rehearse and practice for it in your dream world. Instead of rehearsing all this in the real world, doing it in the dream world is easier. It also allows you to explore the same situation from someone else's perspective and not just your own. So, the next time you find yourself worrying about an interview, turn to your dreams, and things will get easier.

You can also train yourself to speak in front of large groups to get rid of any fear you have. A word of caution: don't try to experiment with too many real-life scenarios. You might reach a stage where you start believing you had done or said something in reality, when all you did was think about it in the dream world. You wouldn't want to be stuck in a situation where you believe you had an important phone call, only to realize it was just a dream.

Once you follow the different tips discussed in this section, you will truly enjoy lucid dreaming. However, be patient with yourself. Lucid dreaming is a skill you need to develop slowly. It can take a couple of attempts, but the results will leave you pleasantly surprised. Before you try any exciting activity, don't forget to ground the dream. After the dream has stabilized, allow your creativity to run wild and explore whatever you want.

Chapter Nine: Meeting Spirit Guides in Lucid Dreams

What Is a Spirit Guide?

Were there instances when you did something that made absolutely no sense, but it turned out to be exactly what you were supposed to do? Such instances often leave you wondering why you acted how you did. If you had such experiences in life, then it's an interaction with your spirit guide. A spirit guide is an entity that holds power and has the energy that it uses to communicate certain thoughts, feelings, responses, and healing to others. Spirit guides radiate positive energy and offer assistance in some form or another. They are known as guides because they assist in a situation by implanting a thought in your head to keep you safe. Spirit guides are also known as guardian angels. You can meet these spirit guides in your dreamland.

Types of Spirit Guides

Spirit guides could be in the form of ancestral guides, ascended masters, a common spirit guide, or even animal guides. An ancestral guide is an entity you have some form of relationship with or who is related to you and your family. It could be a long-dead ancestor or someone you were once close to and is no more. Anyone with your best intentions at heart and who has a kinship with you is often reincarnated as a spirit guide. Your ancestral guides are related to you by blood and are often believed to be guardian angels in different cultures.

An ascended master is an individual who performs reiki or any other energy healing. Ascended masters are physical beings who led a physical life but have moved on to higher planes of energy, such as Lord Krishna, Buddha, or even Jesus. Ascended masters often work with a group of souls and not just individual beings, unlike ancestral guides.

A typical spirit guide is often symbolic or representative of a specific guide and can take on the form of a storyteller, a wise crone, or even a warrior. They usually appear for a specific purpose. The purpose is often to teach you or prompt you to move on a good path. They can also help solve any problems you might be facing. Another common type of spirit guide you might encounter are animal spirit guides. Animal spirit guides function more like companions. For instance, you might meet a deceased pet who was there to help you through the grieving process. According to spiritual traditions prevalent in shamanic and certain Native American cultures, every individual has an animal totem or an animal spirit guide, which helps protect them from negative energies or acts as a guiding light.

Finding Your Spirit Guide

Now that you are aware of what a spirit guide is, try to concentrate on meeting one in your dreamland. There are different techniques you can use to meet one, but don't be disheartened if it doesn't work immediately. As with anything else in life, it takes some time, effort, and patience. Here are some simple tips you can use to find and meet your spirit guide.

Meditation

Meditation is a powerful tool because it helps connect your subconscious with the vast powers of the universe. Before you start meditating to find your spirit guide, ensure your mind is clear of all thoughts and clutter. Concentrate only on finding your spirit guide and nothing else. Don't think of meditation as a destination. Instead, it is a journey. To get started on this journey, visualize yourself in a serene forest, at the beach, a scenic mountainside, or anywhere that relaxes you. Don't think about anything else, and concentrate only on exploring the surroundings. While you start exploring the dreamscape, chances are you will bump into your spirit guide.

As mentioned in the previous section, your spirit guide is an archetype and could come in different forms. The spirit guide's form is merely a representation of certain characteristics and traits you value. For instance, your spirit guide could take on the form of Martin Luther King Jr. It doesn't mean he is your spirit guide but is a representation and embodiment of traits dear to you, such as freedom, resilience, and courage.

Look For Signs

A simple way to meet your spirit guide is to ask for a sign or an omen. Spirit guides sometimes make their presence known through symbols and signs. These symbols, signs, and omens can be quite basic or complicated. All you need to do is merely look for it. Unless you ask the spirit-guide a question, you will not get the answer you need. If you are stuck in a dilemma, ask for a suggestion or a solution, and once you have made your request, start looking for signs.

For instance, if you are considering shifting to a new place, but are scared about it, ask your spirit guide for some guidance. If you notice some signs such as a random conversation with a long-lost friend in the same city you are thinking about moving to, or maybe you notice vehicles with registration plates of the area you're thinking about shifting to, these are signs that can pop up at random times and places. All you need to do is consciously look for them. If you find these signs, it means a spirit guide is reaching out to you.

Dream Journey

A dream journey is quite similar to meditation and is also known as a vision quest. It is essentially a technique used to find your spirit guide via the subconscious mind. Unlike in meditation, where you are awake, the dream journey occurs in your dream state. You are asleep while going on this purposeful journey. Lucid dreaming can help you connect with your spirit guide. Before you sleep, concentrate on your purpose of finding the spirit guide, and focus on what you're trying to accomplish. If you meet someone during your lucid dreams, don't forget to note it as soon as you are awake. Write down your conversations, and all the information you obtain from the other person.

Intuition

Were there instances when a little voice in your head prompted you to do something? Maybe it told you it was time to move on, head in a different direction, or listen to what others said. The little voice that often talks to you is your intuition. Most of us are dismissive of our intuition, but it's quite powerful. The intuitive voice, which guides you in the right direction or prevents you from harm, could manifest as your spirit guide. To identify the presence of the spirit guide, listen to this inner voice, and evaluate the suggestions it gives you. If your intuitive ideas are right and helpful to you, it is your spirit guide trying to connect with you.

There are no hard and fast rules about spirit guides. You might have one or multiple spirit guides who take turns and appear in your life. Remember, a spirit guide appears only in times of need and not whenever you call on them. Unless there is a real need, a spirit guide might not show up, so don't get discouraged.

Connect With Your Spirit Guide

Guidance is always within your reach, but you will not receive it unless you expressly ask for it. If you need help to solve a problem or address a dilemma, ask your spirit guide for their help. The more you ask, the higher are the chances of receiving. It doesn't mean you shouldn't rely on yourself. It merely means you are asking for a little assistance to get where you want . A cab will not stop for you unless you flag it down by waving your arms; likewise, your spirit guides might not reach out to you because you haven't reached out to them. It is not just about asking; be sure that you listen to the advice given by your spirit guides. You cannot listen to them unless you quiet your mind and free up your mental clutter. Once you slow down, it becomes easier to connect with your spirit guide. You can use meditation to attain this objective.

You can ask your spirit guides for assistance by making a note of all the areas in which you need some help. Start with meditation and grab a journal. Write down your problem, ask the spirit guides for their assistance, and start writing down the thoughts that flow into your head. To seek your spirit guide's assistance, you can say something like, "Dear spirit guide of truth, love, and compassion, I welcome you to write through me, so I know what I am supposed to know."

Your job doesn't end here. After you seek guidance, you should also watch out for signs. As discussed in the previous section, spirit guides often offer guidance through different signs, symbols, and omens. Start looking out for these things.

Before you start blindly following the advice you receive from your spirit guides, it's important to test whether the entity you meet in the dreamland is your spirit guide or not. At times, malevolent energies or anyone else invading your dreams might show up as your spirit guide. So, pay close attention to the advice you receive. If you try the advice and nothing good comes of it, that's another sign you shouldn't ignore. Even if your spirit guide looks like your kin or someone you trust, being cautious is a good idea. If all the information you receive from the spirit goes against your beliefs, logic, or common sense, the entity you are interacting with might not be your spirit guide. You will learn more about protecting yourself from negative energies and dream invaders in the subsequent chapters.

Chapter Ten: 14 Things to NEVER Do When Lucid Dreaming

Lucid dreaming is fun and exciting. It allows you to do whatever you want and explore your creativity without any worries. Since you have the power to do whatever you want, it's important to stay in the right state of mind and have good intentions at heart. Even if it is safe, there are certain things you must never try during lucid dreaming. Just because you have the power to do anything you want, doesn't mean you should. The purpose of lucid dreaming is to explore your subconscious; learn, experiment, and explore. So, anything that isn't positive or constructive should be avoided. In this section, let's look at certain things you should never attempt during lucid dreaming.

Mistake #1: No Violence

Lucid dreaming is different from playing a violent video game. Remember, a lucid dream is not an episode of Grand Theft Auto. Every scenario you explore and the different people who feature in these scenarios are all extensions of your persona and subconscious. So, any violence against other entities in your dream is merely a form of self-harm. If you hurt anyone, you are merely hurting yourself, and this is undesirable. Since lucid dreaming is extremely vivid, any physical harm or violence directed towards others could stay fresh even after waking up.

Mistake #2: Lack of Planning

Planning is important in every aspect of your life, and a little bit of planning is important for dreaming, too. If you start lucid dreaming without a plan or a goal in mind, likely you'll merely end up standing there or forgetting what you're supposed to do. Therefore, before you start lucid dreaming, ensure that you have a specific goal in mind. It not only enhances your overall experience but also becomes a learning opportunity. Repeat your goal, right before you go to sleep, or think about it all day long. Once this goal gets embedded into your subconscious, it stays with you even in your dreamland.

Mistake #3: Extremely Exciting Activities

Indulging in extremely exciting activities can end the lucid dream. If your mind is too stimulated, waking up from the dream is quite likely. Before you try to do anything exciting, ensure you have stabilized yourself in the dream world and the dream itself. For instance, if you realize you're lucid dreaming, and your first activity is to jump into bed and have hot sex, it's unlikely the dream will continue. Chances are, you will find yourself wide-awake and restless in the bed. Before you try any of this, ensure that you have some practice over lucid dreaming. Once you've mastered the different techniques discussed in this book, indulging in exciting activities will become easier.

Mistake #4: Shutting Your Eyes

When you shut your eyes in the lucid dream, it awakens you. When you are lucid dreaming, you are viewing and experiencing things from your perspective. By shutting your eyes, you are ending that dream effectively. If your goal is to end the dream and wake up, then shut your eyes.

Mistake #5: Stop Thinking About Your Body

Focusing on the dream and staying in the dreamland when you are lucid dreaming becomes difficult if you keep thinking about your real-life body. If the only thought in your mind is about your physical body lying on the bed, how can you possibly concentrate on the dream? If you want to stay immersed in the dream and wish to reap the various benefits of lucid dreaming, stop thinking about your body.

Mistake #6: Avoid Real-Life Memories

Stop thinking about situations that are quite like your real-life memories or experiences. Here's a simple example: let's assume you are in a lucid dream, and you're talking to a prospective client. You have successfully negotiated the terms of a contract and have cracked the deal. If you are quite elated and happy when you wake up, you might believe the lucid dream was reality, and you cracked the deal. Why does this happen? Lucid dreams are quite vivid, and at times, these memories can get mixed up with your real-life memories. Therefore, the simplest thing you can do is to avoid thinking about memories which are quite similar to your waking life.

Mistake #7: No Bad or Negative Thoughts

Scary lucid dreams might sound intriguing and exciting. Do you want to avoid nightmares during lucid dreaming? If yes, avoid thinking bad or negative thoughts. Remember, a lucid dream is an extension of your subconscious. The simplest way to avoid any negative or bad thoughts from straying into your lucid dreams is to meditate or repeat positive affirmations before sleeping. A positive thought makes for a better lucid dreaming experience. Also, a lucid dream is not an escape or a coping mechanism. Deal with any problems you have in life before you try solving them in the dreamland.

A lot of people use lucid dreams to explore their darkest fears and worries. Or maybe you love the horror genre and want to see if you could survive your favorite horror movie. Initially, it would be best to avoid all negative and scary thoughts. You are in a special state of the subconscious during lucid dreaming. If you don't want to intensify your fears further, avoid thinking about them. You can attempt overcoming your fears once you get the hang of lucid dreaming. If not, you are merely inducing nightmares!

Mistake #8: Avoid Consistent Real-Life Individuals

People you know might feature in some of your lucid dreams. It is quite normal to dream about others you know. However, stop fixating or obsessing over a single person. If someone you know repeatedly appears in your lucid dreams, your mind will create fake memories. As mentioned in the earlier points, you can regulate your subconscious in the lucid dreamland. If you keep hanging out with a specific person in the dreamland, have several conversations, and do things together, your real-life memories become blurred. Your brain would be quite confused when you meet the said person in real life. You might also be disappointed when you don't feel the special connection you did in the dreamland. All this is due to confused memories. As a rule of thumb, avoid spending too much time in lucid dreams with people you know in real life.

Mistake #9: Stop Exerting Too Much Control

You can control and dictate the course a lucid dream takes. Having said that, exerting too much control would take away the magical experience lucid dreaming is supposed to be. If you are just getting started with it or don't have much experience, you cannot exert much control over your dreams. Do not get frustrated if you are unable to control your dream state. It merely means you need more practice to get the hang of it. It takes practice, consistent effort, and a lot of time. Once you're willing to commit to it and make the required effort, you will truly enjoy the benefits of lucid dreaming.

Mistake #10: Avoid Looking In Mirrors

What happens when you close your eyes or think about your real-life body? Both of these things will awaken you. Likewise, looking in a mirror does the same. It might be exciting, and you might be curious about seeing your reflection in a mirror during lucid dreaming. However, try to understand that mirrors don't function like they normally do in real life during lucid dreaming. If you are going to look in a mirror while dreaming, expect it to be different. At times, the reflection in the mirror might be a little scary, and it can wake you. Therefore, understand what you can expect and accept the fact the reflection might be a little scary. Once you are prepared, you will not accidentally wake up. Another likely scenario, you should consider is the mirror could reflect what you are feeling and your general state of mind. If you're in a happy state and thinking positive thoughts, the reflection would be more positive, and vice versa.

Mistake #11: Not Setting A Time Limit

Lucid dreaming is fun and exciting. However, be wary of the time you spend in the dreamland. If lucid dreaming is the only reason you go to bed at night or is the most exciting aspect of your day, something is wrong. As with anything else in life, there needs to be some balance. When unbalanced, things go haywire, and the purpose of lucid dreaming is defeated altogether. Don't use lucid dreaming as an escape mechanism. It is not a coping mechanism to deal with the realities of life. Instead, learn to deal with your worries and use lucid dreaming as a tool for exploring your subconscious. If you spend too much of your time and lucid dreams, you prevent yourself from living life like you're supposed to.

Mistake #12: Not Doing Anything

Not doing anything, merely exploring the dreamland or roaming around, is not a good idea. These activities help stabilize the dream, and that's it. Once you have stabilized the dream, start exploring the dreamland. If you do nothing, you are merely wasting an opportunity. Avoid any constant reality checks while in the dreamland. Enjoy the lucid dream because it is a magical experience. Doing nothing takes away the magic from this experience. It is one of the reasons why you must plan before you start lucid dreaming.

Mistake #13: Avoid Spinning Quickly

Before you attempt to do anything in the lucid dream, the first step is to stabilize the dream itself. A simple way to do this is to spin around in circles. While spinning, do it slowly and only for a while. If you do too much spinning, it might wake you up. To ensure you are dreaming, one or two reality checks will help. Don't go overboard, and don't keep constantly checking to see if you are in the dream state. Spinning too quickly can stimulate your nervous system and wake you up from the dream.

Another thing you should avoid doing is trying to fly when you are not yet ready. It might seem like a cool idea to fly in dreams. After all, we all thought about it at some point or another, and the lucid dreamscape gives you a chance to try it. If you're just getting started, avoid trying to fly. If you try doing it too quickly, your conscious brain kicks in, and you start asking yourself logical questions such as, "How can I fly?" or "I cannot fly because of gravity." These things will wake you up and can lead to a frustrating experience.

Mistake #14: Don't Think, "I Can Do It Later."

If you are aware you are in a lucid dream and feel like doing something, try to do it as soon as you possibly can. Chances are, you'll forget about it if you don't do it immediately. As soon as the lucid dream has solidified, work on enacting your lucid dream script. If you keep telling yourself you can do it later or feel like walking around for a while, you forget about it or, worse, wake up from the dream.

By avoiding these common mistakes, you can enhance your overall experience of lucid dreaming and reduce the likelihood of abruptly waking up from the dream.

Chapter Eleven: How to Protect Yourself While Lucid-Dreaming

It isn't necessary that every dream you have is a pleasant and happy one. You can have nightmares, too. There might be instances when you are lucid dreaming, and something doesn't feel right. Perhaps a disturbing entity or an image somehow entered your dream, and you didn't consciously give it the power to do so. What can you do in such situations? The good news is, there are some simple tips and steps you can follow to avoid any unpleasantness in your lucid dreamland. The two common sources of unpleasantness in lucid dreams are nightmares and dream invasions. In this chapter, we will explore these concepts and learn about tips you can use to protect yourself.

Nightmares

Were there dreams you woke up from with your heart beating rapidly and frantically? Dreams that leave you in a cold sweat? Perhaps you are being chased by a monster while you run to save your dear life. Or maybe you are living through your worst fears while feeling helpless and out of control. Both these instances can abruptly wake you up from your sleep, leaving you feeling anxious.

This brings us to the next point, the differentiation between nightmares and night terrors. Even if they sound similar, they are quite distinct. There are three primary differences between these two concepts. Night terrors often come during the early phases of sleep, while nightmares come at a later stage. Nightmares are often induced when your sleep is the longest, and your dreams slowly turn bizarre and are heavily influenced by the emotions you experience. Night terrors are associated with non-REM sleep, while nightmares are associated with REM sleep. When you have a nightmare, you will likely have a vivid recollection of the unpleasant dream. As far as night terrors are concerned, it's quite likely you'll only remember fragments of your experience or have complete amnesia about the episode.

Nightmares disrupt your REM sleep. It's believed the brain doesn't really stop thinking even while you are asleep. It keeps reviewing all the experiences you had, or memories from different networks that share similar experiences. It also updates certain neural networks and learns to cope with new behaviors even while you're sleeping. This is one of the reasons why you might have nightmares. Any turmoil you experience while you are awake may manifest itself as nightmares during your sleep. Learning to cope with your negative emotions during the waking hours helps reduce the chances of nightmares.

Also, remember, any form of emotional turmoil can cause nightmares, not just fear. There might have been instances when you experience anger, resentment, disgust, or even grief after waking up from a nightmare. Frightening dreams you experience could be the mental manifestation of harm due to perceived threats to your physical or mental safety. Even a threat to your self-esteem, confidence, or sense of security can trigger nightmares.

A simple way to relieve any negative emotion you experience during a nightmare is to rationalize. Lucid dreaming allows you to know you are asleep, and whatever you're thinking about isn't happening in reality. This gives you a simple sense of control. The next time you're stuck in a nightmare, and you're aware of it, think about the situation logically. For instance, if zombies are chasing you in your nightmare, remind yourself you are safe and in your own bed. Another simple technique is to close your eyes to awaken yourself from the bad dream. You have complete control over your brain and thought patterns.

As mentioned in the previous section, one of the common factors that trigger a nightmare is the stress you experience. Your brain actively tries to solve any problem you face, even while you are asleep. Your brain is essentially rehearsing itself to deal with the problem once you are awake. If you can calm yourself before you go to bed, the chances of nightmares reduce. Making simple activities such as yoga, meditation, exercise, a little "me time", or a relaxing bedtime routine can help reduce stress. Lack of sleep or any other form of sleep deprivation can stress your brain, which, in turn, triggers nightmares. Try to sleep and wake up at the same time daily.

To reduce physical and mental stress, stay away from alcohol, nicotine, and caffeine right before bedtime. These substances stimulate the mind. Excess stimulation right before bedtime can send your brain into a hyperactive mode. Another simple technique is to avoid watching any scary movies or reading about any frightening and disturbing events at night.

Another simple way to eliminate stress is by scheduling some worry time. Even if it sounds counter-productive, allocate about five-to-ten minutes of worry time daily. During this period, you can think about every thought that has been worrying you all day long. Instead of ignoring or repressing these negative thoughts, you can create an outlet to deal with them. Once you deal with any unpleasantness, the chances of nightmares will reduce.

When you are lucid dreaming, you have the power to change the script of any dream. If you are stuck in a bad dream, merely change it. To do this, you need first to realize you are in a state of lucid dreaming. For instance, a monster is chasing you in your dream, and you are running in a dark alley. Instead of concentrating on this, think of a happier place. Now, visualize that you are running toward the happier place. After all, you are the master of your dreamland.

Dream Invasion

Did you ever have dreams when you experienced someone else present in there? A foreign presence that wouldn't go away, and influenced the course of your dreams? Or maybe you were in someone else's dream? These things are known as dream invasions. A dream invasion can be an accidental invasion or a purposeful invasion. In a lucid dream, you are either wholly or partly in the astral plane. You are manifesting the dream on this plane, and it temporarily comes into existence. It's only temporary because once you open your eyes, and are fully awake, the dream ends. A dream also disappears if you decide to move away from the astral plane. In a dream invasion, another entity enters the space you've created and interacts with you. Others can invade your dreams via their lucid dreams, rituals, meditation, or even astral projection. Now, let's look at the types of dream invasions.

An accidental dream invasion, as the name suggests, doesn't involve any premeditation. At times, when you share a strong connection with someone, they might get the power to enter your dreamland. In fact, often, all the people involved in the dream are also dreaming. It's similar to a shared dream where someone else is placed in your dream without their consent. The invader has no intention to invade your dream and means no harm. It was merely an accident. Accidental invasions are quite common with empaths. An empath is an individual who can feel and experience what others are feeling and experiencing. If your empathy is high, it's quite likely others would be drawn into your dreams. It's an involuntary experience, and there is no harm in it.

A purposeful invasion is the opposite of an accidental invasion. Why would anyone intentionally invade someone else's dreamland? There are different reasons, and the most common one is to influence the other person's thinking. A dream occurs in the astral plane, and whatever you dream about often stays in your subconscious. Since your subconscious mind is responsible for all automatic responses, including physical and emotional ones, it's quite powerful. Your subconscious memory governs your primary instinct for survival, motivation, and any other emotional reaction. A purposeful invader is trying to control these things by triggering a specific response. A purposeful invader has the power to pull others into their dreams. This is pretty much what the movie Inception is based on.

Another common reason for dream invasion, especially purposeful invasion, is to absorb any emotional energy manifested during the dream state. Lust dreams and terror dreams are the two usual sources invaders use to attain this objective. The attacker absorbs any energy which is created by your body during these dreams.

A dream invasion might sound like a nightmare, but there's a subtle difference between these two things. In a nightmare, it's often your personal stress from real life that's manifested as a bad dream. Not just mental stress, but any physical stress you might be experiencing, such as an illness, pain, or any life-threatening situation could trigger nightmares. Nightmares are often abstract in nature and are usually self-contained. However, in a dream invasion, the nature of the interaction between you and the other being invading your dreams is quite detailed. A nightmare is often illogical because it's a mere manifestation of your fear. A dream invasion is seldom illogical, and you might even have persistent interactions with the other being.

Are you wondering what you could do if you are stuck in a dream invasion?

A dream invasion occurs when someone else has breached your personal energy field. To prevent this, learn to protect your energy field. It's similar to installing a security system on your house to keep yourself safe. A physical security system might prevent thieves and robbers, but a mental security system protects you from negative intentions, feelings, and psychic attacks from malicious entities. To strengthen and protect the energy field, here's a simple meditative exercise you can try.

Start by finding a comfortable spot for yourself. You can either sit down or lie on the floor. Close your eyes, keep your body relaxed, and start breathing slowly and deeply. Take a long, slow, deep breath through your nose and exhale through your mouth. Repeat this ten times or until you feel completely calm. Now, bring up your hands and cupped them together as if you are holding a tiny ball. Visualize that this ball you are holding is full of bright lights. The bright light it radiates is full of love and affection. Visualize this ball is slowly growing until it surrounds you. It's not just surrounding your body, but has spread into the entire space around you. You can see the edges of this ball shimmer like small bright diamonds. Now, hold onto this ball once again and look at how it beautifully glitters. Visualize that you are viewing yourself in this bright light. As you start concentrating on it, the flecks of glitter from the ball are leaving your hands, filling the space between the ball and your body. Take a deep breath and slowly open your eyes. This simple exercise is believed to bring about a sense of serenity and security. You can also perform this exercise in a lucid dream.

Start meditating before you go to sleep at night. Meditation helps enhance your overall energy levels and gives you a chance to access a higher energy plane. It essentially creates a safe environment where the attackers cannot follow you. If your dreams are constantly invaded, don't react or resist them; instead, simply assert your control in the dream world. Remember, your dreams are well within your control, and no one can do anything to you unless you give them the control to do so. Someone else has entered your space, and it is time to reclaim your space. Don't indulge in any conversations; merely disengage. Repeating a simple mantra such as, "You're not welcome here," or "I don't want you here," can effectively end dream invasion.

You also have the power to call on your spirit guide in the lucid dream. Your guardian angel is right around the corner, and all you need to do is merely call it.

Chapter Twelve: Five Advanced Lucid Dreaming Techniques

Lucid dreaming has several positive effects on the dreamer. From becoming more self-aware to developing confidence, the use of dreaming is a wonderful experience. In the previous chapters, you were introduced to a few techniques for inducing lucid dreams. After using these techniques, if you're thirsty for more or are curious to set out on a new adventure, you can use some advanced techniques for lucid dreaming. In this chapter, let's look at these techniques.

Technique #1: Astral Projection

As mentioned earlier, there is a relationship between astral projection and lucid dreaming. When you go on an astral journey, you are essentially projecting your consciousness into the astral world. You are traveling to different experiences and locations in real time without relying on your physical body. In a way, only your consciousness is exploring the different scenarios.

Those who perform astral projections often talk about it as an out of the body experience, almost as if they were ghosts. Astral projection is an intriguing concept, and you can experience it during lucid dreaming. Your dream world is based on your consciousness, while the astral world encompasses so much more than this. It isn't restricted to your personal space or time. It is the culmination of everyone's experiences in life. With astral projection, you can witness and experience events from the past, future, and present. Still, you aren't able to interact with anyone else's internal world. Here are the steps you should follow to explore the astral world during lucid dreaming.

- To get started with astral projection, you need first to enter the state of a lucid dream. To induce a lucid dream, use the WILD (Wake Induced Lucid Dream) method.
- Once the lucid dream starts, shift your consciousness back to the room where you are asleep. Look at your physical body while it's lying on the bed.
- Take a walk around the room and notice any objects you haven't noticed before. For instance, maybe you never paid any attention to a pen you keep in the room. After you have zeroed in on the object, shift all your attention to it. Carefully examine the object and observe every detail.
- After you wake up from the dream, re-examine the object. If the object is not there in the room, or if the details are different, it means you were not astral projecting, and it was merely an extension of your lucid dreams. If the object and all its details are the same, you have successfully astral projected.
- Now that you know how to perform an astral projection, the next time you are lucid dreaming, explore beyond your room. Walk around the house or even the neighborhood. Once you're awake, re-examine the details to ensure it was an astral projection. This is an advanced technique, and you might not get it right at once. Therefore, you need to practice to get better.
- The final test to determine whether you have successfully astral projected or not is to ask your friend to place an object in their house without telling you what the object is. Your friend should tell you where the

object is placed without giving more details. It needs to be in a place that's easily accessible, such as the nightstand, kitchen counter, or the dining table. If you have successfully astral projected yourself, you'll have entered their home and be able to describe the object in detail.

Once you have mastered this technique, you can project yourself to any place in the world. You're not restricted by the physical world's barriers and can traverse between time and space using your consciousness.

Technique #2: Meeting Your Parallel Self

According to the multiverse theory, there are several parallel universes in existence where your parallel selves reside. It is a complex theory, but a simplified version suggests infinite timelines are encompassing several parallel universes. It essentially means that there is a parallel universe where something else would've happened for anything that has happened in your life. It is quite similar to asking yourself how your life would have been had you not made a specific decision at a given point in time. For instance, how would your life have turned out if you did not move to another city? Would things have been different if you chose a different major in college? According to the multiverse theory, for every decision you ever made, there exists a parallel universe, and there are different versions of you living in different timelines.

As with astral projection, you can use lucid dreaming to explore different multiverses of your life. Here are the steps you should follow for this technique.

- Start by inducing lucid dreams by following any of the techniques discussed in the previous chapter.
- Once you are in the state of a lucid dream, concentrate on a specific event or a decision you made in life. Shift all your attention towards the specific experience and meditate on that experience during your lucid dream. Visualize yourself in a parallel reality.

- You can intentionally shift your consciousness to travel on a different path by transferring yourself to the moment and making a different decision. Another alternative is to transport your consciousness into the present moment intentionally but in another reality.
- After you revisit your personal timelines in multiple universes, start visiting alternate timelines of the history we know.
- Don't forget to note all your observations from your visits to the parallel universes after you wake up. It not only helps verify your experience but also makes it more vivid. This technique works brilliantly well because, in your lucid dreamland, there is infinite space and time available. This, coupled with all the unlimited parallel universes that exist, means that there's plenty of scope for exploration.

Technique #3: ALDIT

The Advanced Lucid Dream Induction Technique (ALDIT) is a hybrid technique designed to create an exciting lucid dreaming experience. Here are the steps you should follow.

- Before you start with this technique, try not to consume alcohol, or keep it to the minimum amount. Stay in a positive mood and don't engage in any emotional conflict. Avoid this technique if you are mentally preoccupied or stressed. Altogether, you need at least seven hours of sleep to practice this technique effectively. Before you awaken, you need four hours of sleep, and at least three hours afterward.
- After four hours, wake up and get up from the bed. You can set the alarm to go off if you are unsure whether you can wake up on your own or not.
- (Optional tip: if you want to enhance the overall experience, take 4-8 mg of Galantamine. It's ideal for all those who don't have a sufficient supply of acetylcholine, a neurotransmitter, in the body. This is

especially true for all those who are over 50 years. If you are taking Galantamine, ensure that you eat a light snack and drink some water or fruit juice afterward. If you have any pre-existing health conditions or a cardiovascular disorder, check with your physician before taking Galantamine.)

- Now, it is time to start meditating. You need to meditate for anywhere between twenty and thirty minutes to ensure your mind is free from clutter. Ideally, it would be best if you sat on a chair or sit down on the floor while keeping your back straight and your body relaxed.
- After you make yourself comfortable, it's time to relive a specific dream. Change your response according to what feels appropriate to you right now and see what the result is. Your new response might not show you an actual solution, but it can represent a developmental step towards attaining the final solution. For instance, in one of your lucid dreams, you were faced with an aggressor, but you didn't do anything. Now that you are revisiting this dream, you can assert your authority by standing up to the aggressor. Whatever the dream is, try to respond differently and let it unfold.
- After you have finished reliving the dream, it is time to wake up. You can set the alarm to help you do this. Don't forget to note the new dream after waking up (you can do this immediately or later). Now, it is time to go back to sleep.
- Before you shut your eyes and drift off to sleep, repeat an affirmation about what you desire to do. You can say something like, "I want to become more aware in my dreams and respond appropriately to all the scenarios I face."
- Start counting backward from 100. You might feel drowsy in this process and lose track of the numbers. It

is okay if this happens; allow that drowsiness to take over.

- You might briefly lose consciousness along the way and might feel or hear a vibration. This vibration can appear and disappear; it is also a good sign. If you hear this vibration in your head, concentrate on this energy, and meditate over it. As you start meditating, the energy will intensify. If this energy is present around you, you can also step out of your body for an out-of-body experience. This is known as a WILD (Wake-Induced lucid dream).
- If you don't hear this energy and merely fall asleep, it is known as DILD (Dream-induced lucid dream). If this happens, chances are you will be transferred to a state of lucid dreaming while asleep.

Don't forget to record your observations once you are awake. If you don't want to write it down, keep a digital recorder to record your experience while still fresh in your memory.

Technique #4: Dealing With Fears and Phobias

Fear is an extremely overpowering emotion that can overwhelm you in any situation. Fears are seldom rational, and therefore, giving in to your fear does you no good. Overcoming fears and phobias is not an easy process. The good news is that you can learn to overcome your fears using lucid dreaming. As mentioned repeatedly, in lucid dreams, you have complete control over the scenarios and their outcomes. No one else can regulate your dreams, and the power lies in your hands. If something seems unpleasant, you can put a positive spin on it. There are different techniques you can use to overcome phobias such as hypnotherapy. However, the simplest thing you can do is to tackle your fears in the dream world.

Here is a simple explanation that will give you a better understanding of how you can tackle your fears and phobias in the dreamland. Let's assume that you are scared of snakes. The slimy and slithery creatures trigger a primal fear unlike any other you have ever experienced. Since you have complete control over your dreams, imagine or visualize these scary snakes as cartoon characters. By reshaping how you view the source of your fear, controlling it becomes easier. By reimagining the snake as a cartoon character, you are essentially taking away its power over you. Visualize that you are listening to the upbeat music from a cartoon series. Or maybe you can make the snake talk in funny voices.

The next time you start dreaming, summon a snake. The snake might look a little scary, or it might even be human-sized. Your heart might start racing, and a wave of overpowering anxiety get hold of your rational mind. Merely calm yourself, and remember you have complete control here. The snake will not attack you, and you can make it stop. For starters, why don't you reduce the size of the snake your imagination has conjured up? Next, try replacing it with the memory of a cartoon character. It might relieve a little of your fear and make you feel more empowered. The next step is to talk to this creature as if it were a rational human being. Maybe ask yourself what this snake represents.

Perhaps an accidental encounter in your past created this fear. Maybe it was a disturbing memory. By exploring the cause of this fear, tackling the phobia becomes easier. After a while, if you encounter the same creature in your subsequent dreams, consider exploring the reasons why it scares you. In a way, lucid dreaming is a source of simple therapy. Regardless of whether you are scared of heights, enclosed spaces, public speaking, or anything else, lucid dreaming helps create a realistic yet safe environment to deal with these fears.

Technique #5: Explore Your Personalities

We all have different facets to our personality. A simple challenge you can try to enhance your overall lucid dreaming experience is to conjure different facets of your personality. Why don't you interact with the joker or the philosopher who lies deep within your mind? A lucid dream and anything you experience in it is a mere extension of your subconscious. So, the characters you meet in the dreamland are also extensions of the psyche. Why don't you ask this dream character to tell you a joke that will make you laugh? Even in a two-way conversation with any dream character, you are essentially conversing with yourself. Therefore, if your dream character tells you a joke to make you laugh, you just discovered a side of your persona you probably were unaware of. If a lucid dream makes you laugh, you have come a long way and are getting the hang of lucid dreaming.

Now, it is time to seek out the philosopher within you. A great thing about lucid dreaming is that it helps create a safe environment where you can explore any topic, concept, or idea you want to, without any fears. After all, no harm can come to you when you are in complete control of all the situations and scenarios. If you have ever wondered about your purpose or what your life means, now is the time to explore all this. This might seem like a tricky challenge because you are essentially setting off on a quest to find answers to questions that might not have any answers. Or maybe they do, and now you have an opportunity to find the answers! Either way, it could be a brilliant learning experience. By getting philosophical in your dream world, the answers you obtain from yourself could be quite unexpected. These questions might be too heavy for real-life conversations, but you can safely explore them in your subconscious.

Conclusion

Lucid dreaming is a truly magical experience. It's a type of dream where you are fully aware of the fact that you are dreaming. It gives you an incredible opportunity to explore your dreamland and go on brilliant personal adventures and experiences. It also gives you a chance to reconnect your dreams and interpret them effectively. With lucid dreaming, you are the creator, writer, producer, and director of your own play.

In this book, you were taught the meaning of dreams and their meanings, about lucid dreaming and the different benefits it offers, and different lucid dreaming techniques. The techniques discussed in this book can be divided into two categories: beginners and advanced learning techniques. You were also given a basic introduction to the link between astral projection and shamanic journeying using lucid dreaming. This book also taught you simple tips to prepare yourself for a better lucid dreaming experience and explore your dreamscape. An intriguing concept discussed in this book is how you can meet your spirit guides in lucid dreams and what they could do for you. You were also given practical and simple tips about things you should never do while lucid dreaming and protecting yourself in lucid dreams. When all these topics are put together, it is the perfect book to explore lucid dreaming safely. Once you get the hang of it, the benefits it offers are truly amazing. From enhancing your awareness to better self-control, preventing nightmares, and understanding your power to explore your creativity, you can do it all with lucid dreaming.

As with any other skill, it takes time, patience, and consistent effort. Once you are willing to commit yourself to this process, your efforts will pay off. This book will guide, mentor, and prepare you for a better lucid dreaming experience. With lucid dreaming, you can explore your creativity and delve into your subconscious. Remember, patience is key, and don't get frustrated, even if you stumble a couple of times. It is part and parcel of the learning experience.

Here's another book by Mari Silva that you might be interested in

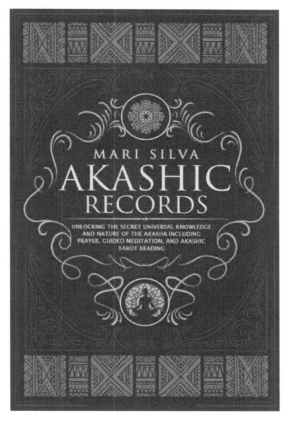

Your Free Gift (only available for a limited time)

Thanks for getting this book! If you want to learn more about various spirituality topics, then join Mari Silva's community and get a free guided meditation MP3 for awakening your third eye. This guided meditation mp3 is designed to open and strengthen ones third eye so you can experience a higher state of consciousness. Simply visit the link below the image to get started.

https://spiritualityspot.com/meditation

Resources

5 Great Benefits of Lucid Dreaming – USA TODAY Classifieds. (n.d.). Retrieved from USA Today website: https://classifieds.usatoday.com/blog/business/5-great-benefits-of-lucid-dreaming/

13 Things You Should NEVER Do In Lucid Dreams! (2019, June 8). Retrieved from www.youtube.com website: https://www.youtube.com/watch?v=bQK4jpeat-Q

40 Things To Do In A Lucid Dream, Especially Number 5. (2018, October 31). Retrieved from HowToLucid.com website: https://howtolucid.com/40-things-to-do-in-a-lucid-dream/

Antrobus, J. S., & Wamsley, E. J. (2009). Lucid Dreams - an overview | ScienceDirect Topics. Retrieved from www.sciencedirect.com website: https://www.sciencedirect.com/topics/neuroscience/lucid-dreams

Barrett, N. (n.d.). How to Lucid Dream. Retrieved from Gaia website: https://www.gaia.com/article/protect-yourself-from-psychic-attacks

Dimitriu, A. (2020, July 5). How to Lucid Dream. Retrieved from wikihow website: https://www.wikihow.com/Lucid-Dream

Ebben, M., Lequerica, A., & Spielman, A. (2002). Effects of pyridoxine on dreaming: a preliminary study. Perceptual and Motor Skills, 94(1), 135–140. https://doi.org/10.2466/pms.2002.94.1.135

Endredy, J. (2018, June 1). Shamanic Dreaming: How to Expand Into Higher Consciousness While You Sleep. Retrieved from Conscious Lifestyle Magazine website: https://www.consciouslifestylemag.com/shamanic-dreaming-lucid/

Hatfield, S. (n.d.). Dream Invasion. Retrieved from Samuel Hatfield website: https://samuelhatfield.com/articles/dream-invasion.html

Holecek, A. (n.d.). Five Benefits of Lucid Dreaming. Retrieved from Kripalu website: https://kripalu.org/resources/five-benefits-lucid-dreaming

Hoppler, W. (2017, September 19). How Guardian Angels Can Guide You in Lucid Dreams. Retrieved from Learn Religions website: https://www.learnreligions.com/guardian-angels-guide-your-lucid-dreams-123964

How to Have Lucid Dreams Easily - Learn Fast & Start Tonight. (2018, July 3). Retrieved from The Sleep Advisor website: https://www.sleepadvisor.org/how-to-lucid-dream/

How to Lucid Dream. (2017, April 18). Retrieved from Gaia website: https://www.gaia.com/article/protect-yourself-from-psychic-attacks

How To Lucid Dream In 2020 (WILD & DILD guides). (n.d.). Retrieved from Lucid Dream Society website: https://www.luciddreamsociety.com/lucid-dream-methods/

Hurd, R. (n.d.). Lucid Dreaming as Shamanic Technology | dream studies portal. Retrieved from https://dreamstudies.org/2010/09/14/lucid-dreaming-shamanism/

Léon D' Hervey De Saint-Denys. (2008). Les rêves et les Moyens de les Diriger : observations Pratiques. Paris: Buenos Book International, Dl.

Lucid Dreaming Frequently Asked Questions Answered by Lucidity Institute. (n.d.). Retrieved from www.lucidity.com website: http://www.lucidity.com/LucidDreamingFAQ2.html

Nunez, K. (2019, May 15). How to Lucid Dream: 5 Techniques, Benefits, and Cautions. Retrieved from Healthline website: https://www.healthline.com/health/healthy-sleep/how-to-lucid-dream#benefits

Nunez, K. (2019, June 17). Lucid Dreaming: Controlling the Storyline of Your Dreams. Retrieved from Healthline website: https://www.healthline.com/health/what-is-lucid-dreaming

Pavlina, E. (2006, November 13). Does Lucid Dreaming Lead to Astral Projection? Retrieved from ErinPavlina.com website: https://www.erinpavlina.com/blog/2006/11/does-lucid-dreaming-lead-to-astral-projection/

Renasherwood. (2011, November 21). Dreaming of Peter: Spirit Guides and Lucid Dreams. Retrieved from Dreaming of Peter website: http://dreamingofpeter.blogspot.com/2011/11/what-heck-are-spirit-guides-and-why.html

Review of Galantamine: The Lucid Dreaming Pill | dream studies portal. (n.d.). Retrieved from Dream Studies Portal website: https://dreamstudies.org/galantamine-review-lucid-dreaming-pill/

Sparrow, G., Hurd, R., Carlson, R., & Molina, A. (2018). Exploring the effects of Galantamine paired with meditation and dream reliving on recalled dreams: Toward an integrated protocol for lucid dream induction and nightmare resolution. Consciousness and Cognition, 63, 74–88. https://doi.org/10.1016/j.concog.2018.05.012

TOP 5 TECHNIQUES TO LUCID DREAM. (2018, June 27). Retrieved from Lucid Dream Society website: https://www.luciddreamsociety.com/top-ways-to-go-lucid-dream-now/

Turner, R. (n.d.). 52 Ways How to Lucid Dream - Mindset, Methods & More. Retrieved from www.world-of-lucid-dreaming.com website: https://www.world-of-lucid-dreaming.com/how-to-have-your-first-lucid-dream.html

Turner, R. (n.d.). Advanced Lucid Dreaming. Retrieved from www.world-of-lucid-dreaming.com website: https://www.world-of-lucid-dreaming.com/advanced-lucid-dreaming.html

Turner, R. (n.d.). Dream Induced Lucid Dreams (The DILD Method). Retrieved from www.world-of-lucid-dreaming.com website: https://www.world-of-lucid-dreaming.com/dream-induced-lucid-dreams.html

Turner, R. (n.d.). Lucid Dreaming Techniques for Beginners. Retrieved from www.world-of-lucid-dreaming.com website: https://www.world-of-lucid-dreaming.com/lucid-dreaming-techniques.html

Turner, R. (n.d.). The Official Lucid Dreaming FAQ. Retrieved from www.world-of-lucid-dreaming.com website: https://www.world-of-lucid-dreaming.com/lucid-dreaming-faq.html

Turner, R. (n.d.). The Cycle Adjustment Technique: Lucid Dreams with CAT. Retrieved from www.world-of-lucid-dreaming.com website: https://www.world-of-lucid-dreaming.com/cycle-adjustment-technique.html

Warnings from Sleep: Nightmares and Protecting The Self. (2017, April 13). Retrieved from Farnam Street website: https://fs.blog/2017/04/nightmares-and-protecting-the-self/

Wigington, P. (2019, April 28). 5 Tips for Finding Your Spirit Guide. Retrieved from Learn Religions website: https://www.learnreligions.com/find-your-spirit-guide-2561603

Wilson, M. (n.d.). The Picower Institute for Learning and Memories. Retrieved from picower.mit.edu website: https://picower.mit.edu/matthew-wilson

What Not to Do in a Lucid Dream - 15 Things (2020) - Lucid Dream Society. (n.d.). Retrieved February 24, 2020, from https://www.luciddreamsociety.com/ website: https://www.luciddreamsociety.com/worst-lucid-dream-ideas/

What is the Difference Between Lucid Dreaming and Astral Projection. (n.d.). Retrieved from www.ennora.com website: https://www.ennora.com/blog/difference-lucid-dreaming-astral-projection/

Printed in Great Britain
by Amazon